GARDEN
Meditations

Brian Butler and Joey Martineck

Foreword
by Jen Settle

Senior Editing
by Aimee MacIver

Content Editing
by Adam Fuselier

GARDEN Meditations

Brian Butler and Joey Martineck

© 2018 Dumb Ox Ministries

Published by Dumb Ox Ministries
316 Girod St., Suite B
Mandeville, LA, 70448
www.dumboxministries.com

Cover by Innovative Advertising
Interior by Russell Graphic Design

Printed in the United States of America

978-0-578-43018-8

To Christian and Gabriel

Acknowledgments

So many wonderful, talented, and committed people in our community help us to shape the outreach of Dumb Ox Ministries. Many thanks to Greg and Lizzy Boudreaux, for their tireless and faithful creative generosity and for saying yes to the adventure of bringing *GARDEN* to life through music.

Heartfelt thanks to Lisa Butler and the Butler family for faithful love in all things and for patient support during the writing of this book.

To Aimee MacIver, for her steadfast work ethic, ninja-like editing skills, and patient sharpening of our writing, as well as her own insightful meditations.

To Jen Settle for her faithful friendship, her prayers, and a beautiful *Foreword*.

To Adam Fuselier for his commitment to excellence, his faithful brotherhood, and his sharp editorial review throughout.

To Dr. Cory Hayes for his precise theological review and helpful suggestions.

To the following people for their insights and reviews of various meditations: Lisa Butler, Lauren Butler, Kathleen Lee, Tyler Pellegrin, Katie Lee, Cortney Eusea, Becki Alford, Cori Carmona, Eric Wilkes, Bob Butler, Sheila Butler, Michelle Kraus, and Michael Kraus.

To all those who formed us in the faith and teachings of St. John Paul II, especially Christopher West and the priests and faculty of Notre Dame Seminary.

To all of the faithful volunteers, benefactors, and intercessors in the community that supports and sustains Dumb Ox Ministries.

Contents

Introduction

Is there any story more familiar than that of Adam and Eve? Their story inspired the musical *GARDEN*, which in turn inspired the book you now hold. Yet even if you haven't seen the play, you will recognize the universal story of our humanity within these pages. This book is a conscious effort to draw every person deeper into that story.

How Joey Martineck pulled off a fresh take on history's most familiar story—without making it outlandish or unfaithful to the biblical account in Genesis—is a wonder. Granted, he had some help from the works of St. John Paul II, who mined the Genesis stories and unpacked them from different angles for years in his talks, books and other documents. St. John Paul II invited us into reflection not only upon the objective facts of creation, but also upon the meaning of the abundant gifts—particularly the gift of our sexuality as men and women—that God first unveiled in Eden.

If you have seen the play, you know that it can prompt some deep consideration of a number of things in our lives. When Archbishop Gregory Aymond first saw the show, he called it "an extraordinary play." He further noted, "I was drawn in spiritually and emotionally as I watched. One cannot watch the play without asking many spiritual questions."

Whether or not you have seen *GARDEN*, these reflections will answer some questions about the Genesis story while perhaps inspiring other questions that have never occurred to you. G.K. Chesterton once wrote, "Our perennial spiritual and psychological task is to look at things familiar until they become unfamiliar again."[1] These meditations are invitations to ponder and reverence the many questions arising from the story of our human family's origin. Pondering these questions in prayer helps the familiar things we have "known" all our lives to become "unfamiliar" and fresh again. When we slow down to reverence the movements of our hearts, while looking to what God has revealed in Scripture, we travel a beautiful path in the garden of our lives, with numerous places to stop, sit, reflect, pray, and grow.

When Joey Martineck sat in my office and proposed the idea of creating a musical based on the story of Adam and Eve in the Garden of Eden, a mix of excitement and skepticism rushed over me. Like me, Joey had been inspired by the writings of St. John Paul II, and he valued the way we at Dumb Ox Ministries had collaborated with Greg and Lizzy Boudreaux in producing their pop album, *To the Dust*. That album featured 13 songs inspired by the three-fold story of man and woman's creation, their fall and redemption, and their call to spend eternity together in Heaven. By the end of our meeting, I had agreed to entertain the possibility of a musical, but little did I know what was about to come. Joey utilized original tracks from *To the Dust* as the creative cornerstones for a new retelling of Adam and Eve's love story. Then, Greg and Lizzy wrote new songs and customized some of their originals for the play. The result became *GARDEN:* a compelling, fresh, fun, hopeful, and artistic musical about what it means to be human.

THE STORIES

Joey and I both love stories. We love reading them, watching them, and sharing them. Story is a powerful medium through which to reflect upon the meaning and trajectory of our lives. Now, three years after meeting with Joey in my office, *GARDEN* re-tells our human story in a way that touches thousands of lives and provokes many questions.

Many of the questions that *GARDEN* inspires were contemplated by St. John Paul II and gave birth to his teaching on the dignity of the person throughout his entire pontificate. His revolutionary insights now known as the "Theology of the Body" first took the form of 135 reflections (129 of them delivered as short talks) given from 1979–1984.[2] As I have studied these writings and shared them with others for the past 15 years, I have found great reward in *remembering* and diving into "the beginning" of our story—our origin. This vantage helps us to understand why Jesus descended into our darkness "in the middle" of our history and made our story into "his-story," clarifying our purpose in life and pointing us toward "the end"—our destiny. As we come to see God's love as our true beginning, middle, and end, we find the grace, hope, and redemption that lead us home.

If we can re-learn the important aspects of all three movements of our human story, then where we came from and where we are now can launch towards where we all want to be. This journey becomes a path of hope and joy, a journey worth taking alongside those with whom we are *most familiar*.

The reflections of St. John Paul II changed my life. By God's grace, we are hearing many people say similar things about their experience of *GARDEN*. But we knew there was a great opportunity to take a deeper step. Like *Theology of the Body* and *GARDEN,* the following 40 reflections are also inspired by the "original love story" of Adam and Eve in Genesis, but they also draw on the many personal stories that compose everyday life.

Joey and I are desperate to share with others the Good News that we have found. With all the darkness in the world today, Good News is deeply needed! The relationship between man and woman is often a place of great hurt, but remains one of great opportunity. St. John Paul II noted, "Human life is by its nature 'coeducational' and its dignity as well as its balance depend at every moment of history and in every place of geographic longitude and latitude on 'who' she shall be for him and he for her."[3] We pray that the balance of the world can shift into greater love by reading, reflecting, and praying about who we shall be for each other in every relationship.

HOW TO USE THIS BOOK

What is Christian meditation? The *Catechism of the Catholic Church* explains, "Meditation is above all a quest. The mind seeks to understand the why and how of the Christian life, in order to adhere and respond to what the Lord is asking. The required attentiveness is difficult to sustain. We are usually helped by books."[4]

This little book endeavors to do exactly that: assist you in your quest to love. This is no easy task, which is why the Church notes it is "difficult to sustain." Thus, this book follows a very simple pattern.

Each meditation begins with a story that leads into insights about life, love, and God's plan for us in relationships. Reflection questions follow to help you pause and engage with what you have read. Again, the *Catechism* is helpful: "To meditate on what we read helps us to make it our own by confronting it with ourselves. Here, another book is opened: the book of life. We pass from thoughts to reality."[5] To foster that transition from insight into real action, each meditation offers a related practical challenge. We invite you to not dismiss some challenges as impractical or "not for me" because the very point is *stretching* ourselves toward living and loving as we were made to do in the beginning! We are confident that within the mix of these 40-plus challenges, everyone will find something fruitful. Finally, we offer a short *written* prayer to invite you into further *unwritten* conversation with God. This conversation with Him is where our greatest opportunities for life and growth are found!

Devoting 40 days to intentional reflection and prayer can be a powerful, concrete step to greater conversion and to becoming more fully the man or woman God made you to be. May you take up these meditations with openness and determination until the story of your own humanity becomes fresh and *unfamiliar* again.

— Brian Paul Butler
  The Feast of the Conversion of St. Paul
  November 25, 2018

Foreword

You may have just witnessed *GARDEN's* retelling of the genesis of humanity. What drama! This is a story of love, joy, unity, temptation, lies, and betrayal, all within the first few scenes! The whirlwind of this drama is not just the story of the lives of Adam and Eve. If we're honest, it's also our own story.

The original drama is played out in our daily lives. We love and enter into union with others; we experience joy; we battle temptations; we fall. When I look at the story of Adam and Eve in the beginning, I long for the peace they experienced. I long for the day when I will be in union with the Lord and with everyone else. This ache and longing draw me closer to the Lord. I also see my own story reflected in Adam and Eve's loss of trust in the Lord and a desire to control how my destiny plays out. It happens every time that I choose my way over the Lord's way, thinking my way makes much more sense or just because it makes me feel good. At the root of that thinking is a lack of trust in the Lord. Do I really trust that the Lord will provide for me? Does He really love me that much? And if I do trust Him, does that make me dependent and vulnerable, things that were frowned upon in my upbringing and in our culture? If I let go of my way, will the Lord really be there? Will He show up like He promised?

Thankfully, I see myself in the story of Adam and Eve's redemption, too. Although in my sin I too am undeserving, the Lord did come for me. The Bridegroom came. Love came!

Love always desires to be expressed, to be made visible, to take on flesh. In a hidden, but no less dramatic way, God's love took on flesh in the womb of Our Lady. The God who is love desired to be seen, touched, heard, and felt. Love took on flesh in order to unite with us—with you. The source of all beauty, the source of all music, the source of all art became one like us in all things except sin. God brought us back into beautiful union and communion with the love we had lost when we turned away from it. With every breath we take, this love woos us back to walk with Him in the garden of our hearts and to experience our trials and joys in union with His.

Whether or not you have experienced the music, story, and characters of *GARDEN*, we all know the joy of love and relationship, the tragedy of temptation and sin, and the hope for redemption. Don't all of our hearts long and ache for happiness that will never end?

When we really look, we see this longing for happiness everywhere. We see the desire for happiness and love at the core of so many movies, theatre, and the arts. We hear it in the haunting lyrics of popular music. We sense it in the cry of the heart that wants to be loved forever—the love we were created for. This is the gift of *GARDEN*. In its music, its writing, and its characters, our search for perfect love is expressed and made visible.

As you embark upon these meditations, you will be guided to deeply reflect upon the joys of love and the ache of loss. You will be encouraged to see your own story within the Genesis story and within the stories of other men and women who struggle with vulnerability, suffering, and transformation. You will rejoice, find connection, and be encouraged to find healing by moving closer to Love Himself.

As you enter into prayer through the stories and challenges found here, turn the eyes of your heart toward Heaven. St. Therese of Lisieux taught that "prayer is a surge of the heart; it is a simple look turned toward Heaven, it is a cry of recognition and of love, embracing both trial and joy."[6] Look to your Creator; if you are open and vulnerable with Him, you will begin to recognize the movement of His love in your life, in both the trials and the joys. You will embrace the stories of your life as moments of grace, love, and beauty.

When we encounter beauty, it moves us to act and to love. How will the Creator's love for you be made visible in the world? Are you willing to trust the Lord as you begin this journey? Will you walk openly in this garden with Him as He draws your heart into deeper union with His?

— Jen Settle
   Consecrated Virgin
   Director of Programs for the Theology of the Body Institute

1

Incarnation

by Joey Martineck

"I'm not flesh and bone like you."

- BRIDEGROOM

When Michael and his girlfriend, Sara, attended a concert in Paris one fall evening, little did they know they would be thrust into the Bataclan terrorist attacks of November 2015. Telegraph News reported that when the shooters began firing into the crowd, a panicked rush to the exits left Michael and Sara trapped inside. Realizing the gravity of their situation, Michael turned to Sara, told her "I love you," and then laid his body over her while bullets soared overhead.

The words "I love you" are important. Saying them aloud certainly matters. But those words take on a profound confirmation when someone actually lays down his body to protect you from harm. The action gives the words "flesh," making the words visible and tangible. Through flesh-and-blood action, love becomes incarnate.

From all eternity, Father, Son, and Holy Spirit have been united in an "eternal exchange of love."[7] Yet "when the fullness of time had come," God the Son took on an incarnate mode of existence (Gal 4:4). In Jesus, the Word of God became flesh—visible, tangible flesh and blood. Even now, Jesus sits at the right hand of the Father in His glorified humanity, in the human body He has for all eternity.

God's love is and always has been unchanging, eternal, and immutable. We have been known and loved by God since before we were conceived in our mother's wombs (cf. Jer 1:5). But what extravagant confirmation of His love has God poured forth by making His love visible in Jesus. He has done this purely for our sake;

God lacks nothing in Himself. Although Jesus no longer walks the streets of Jerusalem, the visible confirmation of God's love endures. In the Eucharist and in the Church, the body of Jesus is still made visible for us. We can touch Him and "know for sure" just how deeply He loves us.

—⚬—

Reflect

In what ways is God's love visible in my life right now?

Challenge

Identify a way to make the words "I love you" become flesh for someone you care about. Examples may include buying your spouse a gift, taking out the trash for your roommate, or writing your sibling a card of affirmation.

Pray

Loving and faithful God, you humbled yourself to take on our flesh in your Son Jesus. Give me the grace to recognize the ways you are making your love for me visible and help me to rejoice in it. Amen

2

Revering the Echo

by Brian Butler

*"There will always be an echo of the Garden in your hearts.
Keep that memory alive as you hope for the Kingdom."*

- BRIDEGROOM

My maternal grandparents, Wesley and Therese, were faith-fully married for 66 years before my Paw-Paw passed away. I hold great memories of visiting them on the weekends in a home defined by real faith and big family.

On a recent visit to Maw-Maw, I went into her backyard and saw the old basketball goal where I had played as a kid. I had risked ankle-sprains with every layup on that goal placed precari-ously on the corner of a raised, cracked concrete slab. Standing there, I reminisced about working alongside Paw-Paw in his old workshop, which he called St. Anthony's Den after his favorite saint. The more backyard steps I retraced, the more memories flooded in. I recalled Maw-Maw's unbelievable pot roast on the stove every Sunday, and Paw-Paw's unforgettable one-liners, like his go-to response whenever I asked what was for dinner: "For you? Wind-puddin' and air-sauce!" He was a strong man, a vet-eran whose courage had earned him a Purple Heart during World War II. But it was Paw-Paw's deep faith that urged him to finish every grace before family meals with, "My Jesus I love you, my Jesus I trust in you."

My grandparents' home was not Eden, and though I can recall adults arguing over politics and kids arguing over who should play with what, my memories are warm and filled with life. My grand-parents had worked hard to create a mini-civilization of love, and my own parents continued this legacy. I grew up in a family culture dominated by grace, rather than by sin, and it has been the firm foundation of my life.

Your family experience may be similarly graced, or it could be very different. Maybe your family is more splintered. Maybe your childhood was filled with heartache and your memories are laced with pain, resentment, anger, confusion, or trauma. But neither your childhood nor mine are *the beginning* of our story. When we take the time to honestly compare and contrast our own experience against the drama of Adam and Eve's life in the Garden, we find rich similarities and differences to be explored for every human family.

I have found that keeping my own earliest family memories alive is best fostered by conversation with my mom and Maw-Maw. I ask questions and listen, and I start to hear an echo of what life used to be like, even within my own family. St. John Paul II taught that the call to make a pure gift of ourselves through the goodness of our bodies as men and women remains hidden within us all. It remains "inscribed in the depth of the human heart as a distant echo, as it were, of original innocence,"[8] that pure state of the heart before it became messy and broken. Why not take some time to ask questions, listening to God and the people who came before you? You'll hear an echo not found in history books and artifacts, but quietly sounding within the walls of your own heart.

—◈—

Reflect

How does my own childhood affect the way I see my life today? How do I currently see my connection to my first parents, Adam and Eve?

Challenge

Ask your parents or grandparents questions about your childhood. Listen well and take the risk to connect the dots of recent memory to better understand your life. Then, share and process what you learned with a friend. Prepare to dive deeply into the rest of this book, prayerfully exploring your earliest origin story in the Garden of Eden.

Pray

Lord, help me to recognize the beauty of the beginning of my story in Eden. Help me better understand and commit the pains and joys of my own personal family history to the care of your Sacred Heart. Guide me into the exact spiritual journey you desire for me. Amen

3

Wonder

by Joey Martineck

"This garden's gazing back at me at last."
- ADAM

On the first day of Maury's sophomore political science class at Texas Tech, a young woman arrived to class ten minutes late. The sight of her left Maury thunderstruck. He listened closely to catch her name from the roll: Dana. As she climbed the aisle stairs to find a seat, Maury turned to his classmate and said, "I'm gonna marry that girl!"

At the time, Maury had a girlfriend, another woman he had been dating for six months. He ended the relationship that afternoon.

Not until the end of the semester did Maury finally work up the courage to ask Dana on a date. That first date eventually grew into a marriage of over 31 years.

Maury has enjoyed many accomplishments in his life, including winning a Super Bowl as a punter for the Chicago Bears. But his NFL championship ring is worth far less to him than the wedding ring Dana placed on his finger. The wonder that enveloped Maury the first time he saw Dana remains one of his most vivid and cherished memories.

Wonder sparked by the sight of beauty and goodness in another isn't just incidental; it means something. These experiences are like echoes of the wonder the first man felt in the beginning upon encountering the first woman.[9] St. John Paul II notes that while Adam's wonder certainly includes admiration for the glory of Eve's body, it extends far beyond into the transcendent wonder of meeting another "*I*" like himself.

Unlike the animals, Eve is able to engage Adam's gaze with one of her own. She not only physically sees him, but *"sees into"* him. Adam recognizes that Eve exists for her own sake, that she comes *from* the Father, just as he does. They are persons created not for any usefulness, but simply for the sake of love. The wonder that Eve stirs in Adam motivates him to serve her, to offer his body to her as a gift. There's no manipulation. There's no thought of what he might be able to gain from her. There is only rejoicing and gratitude that she exists.

—⟐—

Reflect

When have I experienced another person authentically seeing me? How did this experience affect my view of my own worth?

Challenge

Identify some people you see routinely but with whom you don't typically spend much time in conversation (maybe a distant relative, a janitor, or a checkout cashier). Pick one and resolve to offer that person your undivided attention whenever you encounter him or her throughout the week. Practice truly "seeing into" that person and affirm his or her worthiness of love.

Pray

Lord Jesus, you see me and you know me. Help me to experience the reality of your abundant love. Amen.

Crown of Creation

by Aimee MacIver

"You're the latest and greatest, the crown of all creation."

- RED

The Sistine Chapel is a room designed for communion. Here, the cardinals come in union to ask the Holy Spirit to direct the selection of a pope, who will shepherd the Bride, the Church. Here, whenever Mass is offered, Jesus comes in union with His Bride. And here—high above it all on the magnificent, soaring ceiling—is one of the most recognizable images in history: Michelangelo's *The Creation of Adam*.

You can probably picture it now. In it, Adam lifts his hand as the Creator leans down to brush fingertips with the first man. While the focus of the masterpiece flows toward that intersection where the divine and human almost touch, Eve is also present there.

Many have gazed at the depictions of Adam and God without ever noticing her. But look again and you'll see her. She's tucked under God's arm, looking curiously at what God is making, but she's at ease, comfortable. Because she is totally secure in her place with God, Eve looks at Adam without fear, shame, or the strain of competition.

Although Adam is the painting's focal point, the woman is neither in his shadow nor in the background. Before she ever meets Adam, she has her own place near God, and it's a place of unique intimacy. From this intimacy come her identity and the cause of her being. Her unique femininity is critical to the fullness of creation itself. Her dignity springs not just from her function, the sum value of her parts, or even her compelling beauty. The woman is not a supplement or accessory to the man or the Church. She herself is a language, a medium of the Holy Spirit, the Artist. He says through woman what nothing else in creation can say.

What a mistake the culture makes when it batters the woman's dignity by placing false qualifiers on her value, or by demanding that she abandon her femininity as a condition of equality. A common distortion is that real freedom will be found when the woman becomes more like the man, stripping her body of its uniquely feminine gift to receive and shelter life and stripping her heart of its uniquely feminine sensitivities.

We must insist on the bold and glorious truth: God has created woman in His image in a way wholly unique from and wondrously complementary with the man—and this uniqueness is essential to the universe. In our walk toward wholeness, women must allow God to wrap us in His love. Only in His embrace is the security and satisfaction that empowers us to receive another openly and freely as we were created to do.

The uniquely feminine genius cannot be substituted with something different. The Church and the world need women to be women. St. John Paul II says in his encyclical letter to women, "This is a matter of justice but also of necessity."[10] And as one woman, St. Edith Stein, said, the world doesn't need "what we have, but what we are."[11]

—⁓—

Reflect

What false conditions on a woman's dignity have I experienced, seen, or even participated in? What are some unique gifts of the feminine genius?

Challenge #1

Find a copy of Michelangelo's painting. Ponder the visual of Eve tucked in God's embrace, and allow new insights about authentic femininity to arise from your contemplation.

Challenge #2

Read St. John Paul II's 'Letter to Women,' in which he thanks women for the vast diversity of their gifts and irreplaceable contributions to the human family.

Pray

Lord, you have made woman with her own unique and unrepeatable dignity, design, and gifts. Help me to first see and understand them, and then to have the courage to live and honor the truth. Amen.

Serving

by Joey Martineck

"I won't serve."

- SERPENT

Luisa and Jimmy were overjoyed upon learning that they were expecting their first child. After a lot of research, they planned an all-natural childbirth. When the day came to deliver their baby, however, complications arose and Luisa's cervix had difficulty dilating to the necessary degree for safe delivery. Twelve hours of labor turned into 24 hours . . . and then 36 hours of labor. Still, her body was barely any closer. Doctors tried several expediting drugs without success until Luisa had been laboring for more than *56 hours*. The grueling labor finally ended with Luisa being transferred to surgery for a C-section.

Thankfully, both Luisa and their baby are happy and healthy today. But Jimmy says he will never forget the shocking sight of Luisa immediately after the C-section. Her arms were extended from her sides as she lay in a pool of blood. This vivid image is what Jimmy now recalls every time he goes to Mass and hears the priest pray, "This is my body given up for you."

In freely giving up His body for us, Christ demonstrates that true love involves sacrifice at the service of another. The Second Vatican Council declares that "Christ fully reveals man to himself and makes his supreme calling clear."[12] Christ shows us what it means to be human. He not only reveals the Father to us, but also reveals "us" to us. Our supreme calling is to pour ourselves out for another, to lay down our lives for another like Jesus did for us on the cross.

Scripture says that "by the envy of the devil, death entered the world" (Wisdom 2:24). According to Catholic tradition, at the moment of their creation the angels were given a choice to serve God or refuse Him for all eternity. When some of the angels foresaw part of God's plan for humanity (and perhaps even foresaw elements of the Incarnation), they rebelled against God. Though these fallen angels (now known as demons) entice us to join their refusal to serve, we are called to give as Jesus did—never from force or compulsion, but in total freedom. And in this service is a glorious paradox: by losing our lives, we find the fullness of life itself (cf. Matt 16:25).

I was once acting in a play that required combat choreography for which I had to perform a flip. For weeks I tried to execute the flip without success. Scared of falling the wrong way and getting injured, I held back and did not throw myself wholly into the movement. But ironically, holding back in fear of injury actually *caused* me to fall incorrectly and get hurt every time. The only way to avoid injury was to go all-in. When the director eventually remarked she might just cut out the flip altogether, I got mad. I did the flip again—but this time I finally committed to it, despite my fears. For the first time, I landed perfectly and never got hurt again.

When God calls us to service and self-gift, we may feel a fear of suffering that makes us hold back. Though everything within us might be screaming, "Run away! Save yourself!," if we wholly commit to the Lord, we will find life!

—⟡—

Reflect

Who is God calling me to serve at this time?

Challenge

Do an act of service for someone that involves a degree of personal sacrifice. Tell no one about your service and do not complain. Then later, reflect in prayer on how your choice to serve sacrificially has brought new life.

Pray

Loving and faithful God, I am scared to serve. Give me confidence in you when it feels like I am being asked to give more than I can. Help me to serve you and others out of gratitude for your great love for me. Amen.

Sheer Goodness

by Joey Martineck

"All I see is a lonely king"

- SERPENT

In Caird and Schwartz's musical Children of Eden, the show begins with these lines from the Father (God):

I dreamed a perfect garden, And there were whirling shapes, And swirling sounds, And I wasn't lonely anymore.

Though *Children of Eden* it is a great work of art, in many ways, I wrote GARDEN as a response to some of the ideas it conveys, ideas many of us have been confused about.

God did not make man and woman because He was lonely. The very first sentence of the *Catechism of the Catholic Church* describes how "God, infinitely perfect and blessed in Himself, in a plan of sheer goodness freely created man to make Him share in His own blessed life."[13] The Father, Son, and Holy Spirit are wrapped up in an eternal mutual exchange of love. No human description can capture the glorious communion that exists within the Trinity.

It's important to note that God is not another "thing." He is not just a "bigger and better" version of us. He is the uncreated source of all that exists. According to St. Thomas Aquinas, since God is complete in Himself, lacking nothing, He does not want for anything.

The reality is: God has no need for us. While this statement may strike us as harsh, it actually reveals a wonderful truth: God *chooses* us.

Through the Cross, God has made clear that He does—mysteriously—desire us. He desires us in the sense that he wants us to possess what we lack, union with Him. Far from being "apathetic," God's care for us flows from his unchanging nature. He is not moved by fleeting attractions or repulsions. Ultimately, we are the ones drawn to Him, as the source of all Goodness.

—⁂—

Reflect

How does it make me feel to know that God does not need me, but He wants me?

Challenge #1

Read the Catechism's entire first paragraph referenced above. You can find the text online if you do not have a hard copy. Use this paragraph as a source of contemplation on God's sheer goodness. .

Challenge #2

If you sometime struggle to believe God chooses and desires you, meditate in silence before a crucifix on the words Jesus spoke from the cross: "I thirst" (Jn 19:28). To dig deeply into this mystery, read St. Teresa of Calcutta's letter "I Thirst for You," which can be found online.[14]

Pray

Father, Son, and Holy Spirit, you are perfect. In you is the ecstasy of unspeakable communion and love. Draw me into your eternal communion. Amen.

Freedom

by Brian Butler

*"Why would you put something
so awful in the Garden?"*

- EVE

I imagine that when Eve first felt the "intensified pangs of her childbirth" (cf. Gen 3:16), she regretted eating from that forbidden tree. My guess is that she soon asked the big question that humanity has pondered ever since: *Why did God give us freedom in first place?*

This question draws us directly into the interplay of free will, desire, our opportunity to love, and the consequences that follow when we fail to love. All this existential depth hangs upon the tree of the knowledge of good and evil. That tree is no longer within Eden, but grows within the center of our own hearts where we wrestle with the gift of our freedom. The *Catechism* reminds us, "The heart is our hidden center . . . the place of decision . . . the place of truth, where we choose life or death."[15]

While still a young theologian, Karol Wojtyla, who would later become Pope John Paul II, wrote that "Freedom exists for the sake of love."[16] This means that wherever love exists, freedom is also there: it is a "pre-req" for love. Without freedom, love cannot exist at all; in fact, freedom itself exists so that we can make the right decision to live *for* someone in the right way.

Our freedom is good, but the consequences that come from misusing it can be awful. It's simultaneously terrifying and exhilarating to exercise the gift of our free will. It's surfing on a tsunami. It's laying down our life for a friend and not knowing if he or she will even notice. It's offering money or food to the beggar on the street. It's leaning in for the kiss at the altar. It's whispering 'I love you' for the first time with our hearts pounding in the dark, awaiting a reply. It's facing temptation when we are alone and choosing what no one else will ever see. Will we use our freedom to choose the fullest good, or to choose what God has revealed to be bad (and forbidden) for us?

The *Catechism* tells us, "Freedom makes man a moral subject ... Human acts, that is, acts that are freely chosen in consequence of a judgment of conscience, can be morally evaluated. They are either good or evil."[17] When we choose against God's commands, we commit a moral evil, working against God and his people. Morally evil acts cause division where God intends unity—for example, in our families and communities. Whether we see it or not, every individual choice enacts a chain of cause-and-effect that ripples throughout the human family. The whole human family shifts off-balance whenever its members choose the forbidden fruit. Conversely, whenever we freely choose the good and act to love God, family, and neighbor, the human family is healed one choice, one relationship at a time.

In many Scriptures, the choice is clear: "God in the beginning created human beings and made them subject to their own free choice ... Set before you are fire and water; to whatever you choose, stretch out your hand" (Sir 15:14, 16). This truth repeats in Deuteronomy: "I have set before you life and death, the blessing and the curse. Choose life, then, that you and your descendants may live" (Dt 30:19). The choice—freedom—is up to you and me.

So, why would God put something like that in the Garden? To give us the opportunity to use our freedom in the way it was intended, to say yes to Him in total trust that His way is best, and to love in the way that He intended. When we do so, our freedom will become a source of life for us and our families.

—ᴍ—

Reflect

Have I considered why God did not make me a robot, programming automatic responses from me? What does it say about the Father's love that He created me with total freedom to reject or love Him, to reject or love others?

Challenge

Pause and ponder before every choice today, even the smallest and most routine. In this exercise, appreciate the powerful gift of your freedom and resolve to use it to love well.

Pray

Dear Lord, thank you for the wonderful gift of my freedom. Help me appreciate it more consciously today and do all I can to mature in freedom and choose to love you. Amen.

Gift

by Joey Martineck

"Adam is the best, best, best gift you ever gave me!"

- EVE

One night during my college days at Georgia Tech, I was talking with my friend Frank on the phone. He had recently graduated and started working full-time in Louisiana, but often came back to visit Atlanta where his girlfriend, Heather, still lived. Before hanging up, Frank mentioned to me that he was getting ready to make the trip to Atlanta that night. I checked the clock. Concerned at the late hour, I asked, "Frank, that's an eight hour drive. Are you sure you won't fall asleep on the road?"

Frank's voice got very serious. "Oh no, Joey. There's no need to worry about that. Just the thought of seeing Heather's face in the morning is enough to keep me awake all night long."

I should point out that Heather wasn't listening on another line. Frank wasn't trying to score brownie points. We were just two guys talking. From the sincere depths of his heart, Frank had shared what he truly saw in Heather: gift.

St. John Paul II says that the "freedom of the gift—the disinterested gift of self . . . allows both the man and the woman to find each other reciprocally."[18] In the beginning, Adam and Eve are naked yet feel no shame. This freedom exists because they behold each other wholly as gift. What they see in each other's bodies is the Father's personal plan of love for each of them. In this way, their nakedness is both physical and spiritual. The body reveals the truth about the person. Who Eve really is—her deepest, most definitive identity as a beloved daughter of God—is visible through the body to Adam (and vice versa).

In our fallen humanity, we often enter into relationships hoping, perhaps subconsciously, to gain something. But we would be wise to heed an old Christian axiom: "You cannot give what you do not have." I can't truly enter into a relationship in which I give love if I haven't first received love. It is only because Adam has first entered into an intimate relationship with the Giver (God) during his solitude that he is later able to recognize and receive the gift of Eve.

This is the true meaning of self-mastery, which many mistake for mere denial or repression. Self-mastery does involve saying "no" to many attractive things in life. But if all we are doing is saying "no," then we may be slipping into prideful rigidity. Our "no's" have value only when said for the sake of "yes!" to something far more beautiful: God and the gifts He loves to lavish upon us.

—◊—

Reflect

Do I see the relationships in my life as gifts or burdens?

Challenge

Spend time cultivating gratitude by thanking God for three to five different relationships in your life. Be concrete about what you are grateful for in these relationships. Be intentional about how to make your gratitude more visible.

Pray

Lord Jesus, in your prayer to the Father, you said that we were the Father's gift to you. Give me courage to see myself as a gift, someone you will to exist, and help me to see others in the same way. Amen.

Remembering

by Brian Butler

"I ruined paradise for everyone"

- EVE

When I was 17, I worked for a friend's father who owned a small electrical company. I delivered tools to job sites, dug ditches, and did whatever else was needed. Mr. Brinklund was a good man who gave clear instructions. One of his directions was always to walk around the company truck before driving away from a job site, checking that all the bins were closed and secure. One day I forgot. I arrived at the next site with a side-bin door wide open and a fairly expensive sump pump missing. Apparently, it had bounced out somewhere along the way.

I was distraught. How could I have forgotten the simple and important task entrusted to me? How could I face Mr. Brinklund? When I told him what had happened, he smiled and told me it was okay. I repeated that I was sorry; he repeated his forgiveness and suggested I learn from the mistake and move on. But I couldn't. I hung my head and made a big deal of it, mumbling about how stupid I was.

That's when Mr. Brinklund invited me to sit down and then taught me a short lesson.

He smiled at me with tender eyes, asking why I was so upset. *Why?* I had been irresponsible, lost an expensive tool, made a mess of my job, and disappointed him. He patiently repeated that he had already forgiven me, and that his company could easily replace the tool. Then he asked why, if I believed *he* had forgiven me, could I not forgive myself?

My memory had been hijacked by pride that gripped onto my mistake so tightly that it couldn't grasp Mr. Brinklund's forgiveness. I had *heard* but had not truly *received*. Convinced that my mistake had revealed the real "me," I found his mercy harder to receive than the self-accusation that gnawed at me.

The enemy of God (Satan) often attacks us in this way. He attempts to accuse us and remind us of our sins in order to prevent us from receiving mercy. He lies to us, saying that our sins confirm our fear that we are not worthy. It's been said that Satan forgets our names and calls us by our sins, but God forgets our sins and calls us by our names.

Jesus Christ said, "If you remain in my word, you will be my disciples, and you will know the truth, and the truth will set you free" (Jn 8:32). The truth is that we are sons and daughters of a God who loves us and is ever-ready to restore us. We are set free when we make choices from this truth rather than from the memories of our sins. We are set free when we not only hear, but also receive. St. John Paul II said Christ's words are meant to help us remember the truth about our humanity—that our *deepest* inheritance is not the darkness of original sin, but the fullness of life.[19]

—✴—

Reflect

What habits cause me to forget who I really am? Pray silently for God to reveal one truth that could be part of the "deeper inheritance" which you have been resisting or forgetting.

Challenge

Recall a moment when you failed and a moment when another person failed you. Ask God for grace and a plan for how to approach the other person and yourself with forgiveness and mercy.

Pray

Lord, remind me today of your love and fidelity in the beginning which is deeper than the sinfulness I have inherited. Silence the accuser and help me to receive the "deeper inheritance" that I have forgotten or resisted. Amen.

Attempting to Earn Love

by Joey Martineck

"How can I give you what you won't freely receive?"
- BRIDEGROOM

I spent many Sundays growing up watching NFL football with my dad. One day, we played a special card game that was designed to be played while watching a football game. For example, if a player held the touchdown card and a touchdown occurred in the televised game, he scored five points.

Halfway through our game, my dad caught me cheating. Instead of yelling at me or punishing me, he just looked at me with tremendous sorrow in his eyes. We never played that game again.

I'm not sure exactly why I wanted to win so badly. It may sound silly, but I think I genuinely believed that I could impress my dad if I won. Instead, by trying to earn my dad's love, I spoiled the gift my dad was actually giving me: quality time shared between father and son.

God's love is not a reward or a prize to be earned. In following Christ, we must recognize that it's "not that we have loved God, but that He loved us and sent His Son as expiation for our sins" (1 John 4:10). God loves us first. In developing the character of Serpent in *GARDEN*, I found inspiration from the older brother in Jesus' famous parable of the prodigal son. The older brother in the parable cannot understand that his father's love is free. Jesus uses this story to remind us all that the Father's love is not the product of our efforts. We are already loved.

If we are hoping to earn God's love from our good works, we are mistaken. The very attempt may actually block us from receiving what we desire. Therefore, our acts of service, our love for God and others, should flow from gratitude, as a response from being so greatly loved. If, however, our good works are driven by an attempt to curry favor with God—out of fear of losing it or a desire for some future reward—we may find ourselves like the older brother in the parable. We may be left feeling bitter at the mercy God lavishes upon sinners, and miss the gift He offers.

—m—

Reflect

If I look honestly at my heart, is there anyone whom I believe is unworthy of God's love?

Challenge

Identify a religious practice you find burdensome. Next time before undertaking it, spend a few minutes reflecting on how the Father beholds you with delight.

Pray

Loving and faithful God, thank you that your love for me is not conditional. Thank you that your love is deeper than my pious practices, my sins, my successes, and my failures. Help me to believe that being your child is enough. Amen.

Take a Nap

by Brian Butler

"Trust me. Take a nap. It'll be worth it."

- BRIDEGROOM

Has anyone ever done something kind and loving for you while you slept? One Christmas morning, I awoke to discover my very own field goal posts in my backyard. My dad had made the wooden posts and installed them into the ground with a manual post-hole digger late on Christmas Eve, when the outdoor temperature was 27 degrees. Joy beyond all measure filled my nine-year-old heart when I saw the set on Christmas morning, magnified by the sense that they had magically appeared while I slept.

We are vulnerable when we sleep. We lose our awareness of everything happening in the world around us. But this vulnerability also presents unique opportunities to love. When someone surprises us with a gift while we sleep—breakfast in bed, an amazing Christmas gift, or some other thoughtful surprise—we are astonished and overwhelmed with gratitude because we did *nothing to earn that gift*, and had no inkling of its existence until the moment we are face-to-face with it. The timing and the surprise of the gift magnifies the generosity of the giver.

St. John Paul II notes "there is no doubt" that Adam fell asleep yearning to encounter another like himself. If sleeping connotes dreams, John Paul supposes that Adam's longing for a "second I" filled his dreams.[20] Even as Adam hoped for and dreamed of one to whom he could give himself, he could not yet fathom the magnitude of what God had planned. He rested and waited with zero knowledge of how God would reach into his vulnerability and fashion the one who, like Adam, would also be made from God's love and in God's image—the one who could be his true partner in self-gift.

So often we don't trust God and don't want to rest or wait for anything. We want our desires fulfilled now. We grasp at achieving them by ourselves. We reject fruitful waiting for immature impatience. Taking a nap? Being vulnerable to God's unknown plan? *No way,* we say. *I'll make my own breakfast in bed. After all, I know best how I like it. Better to just take control for myself.*

But before and after God created the animals, Adam stood alone before God in a unique and unrepeatable relationship with him. Through his body, man discovers he is fundamentally different than the animals. In this *original solitude,* he discovers himself in a "unique, exclusive, and unrepeatable relationship with God himself" as a "subject of the covenant" and a "partner of the Absolute."[21] Adam was not merely waiting *for* something or someone else. He *waited with* and *rested in* peaceful relationship with God.[22]

God our Father knows us better and loves us better than even our parents, spouses, siblings, or children. He calls us to rest in the reality that He constantly works for our good, preparing good things for those who love Him (cf. Rom 8:28). Adam's nap reminds us that if we trust God and simply rest, we will see He's even better at gift-giving than we could hope for.

—⟋ᴍ⟍—

Reflect

What is something I yearn for that has not yet been fulfilled? What if God is waiting for the perfect timing to fulfill this desire for me? How does this possibility change how I approach or enter into the waiting?

Challenge

Meditate on God's word as you lay down to take a "nap of trust," not merely to recharge physically, but also to practice patiently waiting, resting, and deeply trusting in the dreams He has planned for your life.

Pray

Lord, help me to rest in your faithfulness today and trust in your perfect timing. Open my heart to be vulnerable to you, so you can give me what you want to give, exactly when you want to give it. Amen.

Vulnerability

by Joey Martineck

"Why would you be afraid to tell me how you really feel?"
- BRIDEGROOM

I've battled anxiety and depression my whole life, but only recently have been able to give it that name. My first few years after college marked some of the toughest struggles. Moving to a new city far from my family, working a demanding job with lots of travel, and learning how to "adult" added extra stress I didn't know how to handle.

During this time, I went on a young adult retreat titled "Longing for More" hosted by Dumb Ox Ministries. I thought it no coincidence that my friend Greg Boudreaux was there, a friend I had previously come to know through other ministry work.

At one point during the retreat, I went out to walk and pray. I realized that my life was in a really bad place and in the moment, my heart cried out to God. A few yards away, Greg was tossing a football with his friend Brian Butler, whom I had not yet met personally. The ball landed near me after an overshot, so I tossed it back to Greg. He must have noticed the look on my face because he immediately asked me how I was doing.

I could feel the canned response coming: "everything's fine." But instead I blurted out, "It's been really hard." And then I broke down.

Brian joined us. They both talked, listened, and prayed with me. I felt incredibly exposed, but the way they gently received my hurting spirit made me feel safe. Most of my interactions with other men in my sales career were cutthroat and competitive.

Greg and Brian showed me true brotherhood, seeking not to tear me down but to build me up. They each shared distinct words with me. Brian prayed: "Give him the courage to take risks." Greg heard from the Lord: "Harmony."

Being vulnerable with these men was scary, as vulnerability often is. It opens the possibility of being rejected or hurt. Yet without vulnerability, we can never experience genuine connection and intimacy with others. My moment of vulnerability with Greg and Brian led me to desperately needed healing that would not have existed if I had given into the urge to hide behind a canned response.

That moment continued to bear fruit three years later as the three of us met again not in the grass of a retreat center, but in the first planning meeting for the original production of *GARDEN*.

—⚭—

Reflect

How much do I struggle with vulnerability? How has this affected my relationships and even my own healing?

Challenge

Seek out community. Find a small group of people of your same sex. Allow vulnerability to build true sisterhood and brotherhood among your group. If a group is not available to you, try being more intentional with a few trusted friends. Take advantage of opportunities to open up to those who have earned your trust.

Pray

Lord Jesus, you know what I carry around inside my heart. Bring it to the light in healthy ways. Allow me to let myself be seen by others. Amen.

13

Love Is

by Brian Butler

*"I choose to love you more each day, no matter what
the others say . . . my love is staying still."*

- EVE

Dave Roever was a Texas teenager who liked to work on cars.
His Christian family raised him to believe in faithfulness to
God, family, and country. The girl he liked, Brenda, felt he was
over-zealous when one day he told her in the school hallway that
he loved her. She slapped him across the face, telling Dave never
to say it again unless he really meant it.

A few years later, after dating with purity and showing true
love, Dave and Brenda married. Shortly after their wedding, Dave
was drafted into U.S. military service during the Vietnam War.
Selected as a member of the Brown Water Black Beret, he trained
with his unit for special warfare by the Navy. After rigorous river
patrol training, Dave spent a ten-day break at home with Brenda.
On the day of his departure for Vietnam, he kissed her and promised, "Baby, I'll be back without a scar."[23]

Dave flew to Sa Dec, south of Saigon, where he joined River
Division 573 and served on the front lines against the Vietcong.
In the eight months that followed, he held onto his faith. While
many others gave in to drugs, pornography, or prostitutes, Dave
stayed true to his vows.

On July 26, 1969, near the border of Cambodia at Thu Thua,
Dave's unit moved upriver to surveil an area in which there was
an intense firefight the day before. As the boat slowed and headed toward the bank in an eerie stillness, suddenly Dave sensed

something was wrong. He grabbed a white phosphorus grenade, pulled the pin and cocked his arm to throw it, intending to create a smokescreen for his boat to make a getaway. At that exact moment a sniper shot Dave through the back of his hand, striking the grenade. Blinding light flashed. Burning at 5,000 degrees, the grenade exploded only inches from Dave's face.

With his body in flames and the right side of his face destroyed, Dave jumped into the water and managed to swim to shore, where he collapsed, still on fire. He was rescued and rushed by helicopter to Japan for treatment. After some recuperation, he was eventually sent back to San Antonio.

The soldier in the bed next to Dave was skinless, severely burned from head to toe. When the soldier's wife came in, she tossed her wedding ring at his feet and said she could never walk down the street with him again. Then, she left.

Watching was Dave—a mangled shell of the man who had kissed Brenda goodbye eight months earlier. All he could do was wait in fear. Finally, Brenda arrived. Unable to identify Dave by appearance, she approached his bed and checked the nametag on his arm. Then, she bent down and kissed him. *On his face.* "I want you to know that I love you," she said, as she looked him in his one good eye. "Welcome home, Davey."[24]

Brenda stayed that day as long as the hospital allowed her. Through her heroic love, hope rose in Dave's heart as he experienced love in a way he never imagined on his wedding day. Brenda's "I do" became a daily commitment. She meant her vows, and she fulfilled them. As time passed, Dave's body remained disfigured and Brenda's love remained faithful. Decades later, they shared life with children and grandchildren, the enduring fruit of their faithful love.

Their marriage was made in heaven, strengthened in war, and etched in the faithful vows of a love that burns deeper than any grenade and louder than any scars.

—ᴍ—

Reflect

What most tempts me to leave when God calls me to stay faithful to my promises? What situations am I facing that tempt me to run away? How am I like Dave, living in fear that Our Lord will come to my bedside and disown me because of my sin and brokenness? In moments of despair, do I cling to the hope of His great fidelity? On the other hand, who in my life may be fearing my rejection?

Challenge #1

Ask God to reveal a time that you, like the wife of Dave's hospital roommate, may have rejected someone because of your own insecurities. Ask God to help you repent and restore that person's hope by your actions and/or prayer.

Challenge #2

Has someone loved you heroically? If you are able, remind this person of how much this meant to you and offer prayer and sacrifice for his or her intentions. Share this important moment with someone else today.

Pray

Lord, help me to remember that fidelity to my promises is a reflection of your faithful love. Fortify me, Holy Spirit, that I may be faithful to my promises. Help me be faithful, as you are. Amen.

14

The Sign of Marriage

by Joey Martineck

"It's written on their skin"

- BRIDEGROOM

In *The Legend of Zelda: Ocarina of Time,* a golden triangle known as the "Triforce" contains the power of the gods that keeps the world in harmony. When the Triforce tragically breaks into pieces, each part is given to someone chosen by destiny, even without his or her own knowledge. These chosen ones bear the Triforce mark on their bodies, specifically on the backs of their hands.

Our bodies, too, bear a mark—a divine imprint. The physical design of our bodies reveals that we are made for "another." St. John Paul II calls this revelation the "spousal meaning of the body".[25] From the moment of our creation as male and female, God began telling us a story. Through the design of our bodies, God has been revealing the nature of Christ's love for us and—even more mysteriously—the nature of the Trinity as a communion of persons.

Have you ever noticed that the Bible opens and closes with marriage? Christopher West often points out how in Genesis, we see the marriage of Adam and Eve, and in the Book of Revelation, we see "the marriage supper of the Lamb," an analogy for the marriage of Christ and the Church (Rev 19:9 RSV-CE). Earthly (natural) marriage is a sign (or icon) of our ultimate destiny: heavenly "marriage" which fulfills our deepest longings. It is a beautiful gift when a man and woman get married, but this kind of marriage is not our highest or ultimate goal. Because every human person—young, old, married, single, consecrated, ordained, male, female—is destined for heavenly marriage, earthly marriage is a sign for everyone, not just those called to the Sacrament of Matrimony.

St. Paul expands on this idea when he says that "'a man shall leave his father and mother and be joined to his wife and the two shall become one flesh'. This is a great mystery, but I speak in reference to Christ and the church" (Eph 5:31–32). What is the "great mystery" of marriage? That the earthly union of man and woman sheds light (analogically) on the even more glorious union of Christ and the Church. Christ the Bridegroom desires to unite with us and fill us—His bride, the Church—with life!

When my friends Ross and Elizabeth got married, they made their wedding vows hand in hand with a crucifix between their palms. Why? Because the cross reveals the true meaning of marriage. Spouses are called to lay down their bodies and pour themselves out for the other self-sacrificially like Jesus did.

With earthly marriage containing the power to illuminate the "great mystery" of Christ's love for us, should we be surprised that marriage is under spiritual attack? Consider the Serpent's vow in GARDEN to twist the union of Adam and Eve. We certainly see many distortions of the sign of marriage today, but imagine how amazing it could be if the world had a clear, true understanding of the body and sexuality lived according to God's original design!

—⁓—

Reflect

Do I view my spouse (or future spouse) as someone to serve or as someone who ought to serve me? How well do I grasp marriage as a call to service? What marriages have I witnessed that truly illuminate the spousal analogy?

Challenge

Fasting is a powerful tool not only for focusing our prayer, but also for restoring order to our passions. It fosters growth in virtue and love of

God. Fast for a day for your spouse or future spouse, your vocation, or those you are called to serve. Remember that fasting may take non-dietary forms if you have medical restrictions; for example, you can fast from a hot shower.

Pray

Lord Jesus, you laid your body down while we were sinners, before we said sorry. Reveal to us the true meaning of marriage as you created it to be. Amen.

15

To the Dust

by Brian Butler

*"When our dreams were washed away/
Our fear of losing them could no longer stay."*

~ ADAM & EVE

Antonio had been married to Emily for just over two years when she was diagnosed with stage 4 brain cancer. Even after extensive treatment, the cancer relentlessly attacked this bright young woman's feminine features, and months later, she now lay in her broken body, sleeping in a hospice bed and awaiting the inevitable. As I approached their home to visit, I noticed an inflatable Grim Reaper decoration in the yard next door. Its long, white fingers gripped nothing but air.

After Antonio and I had talked a while, Emily stirred awake enough for us to pray with her. She could not speak, but she smiled weakly when Antonio kissed her on the head and blessed her with holy water—all over her ears, mouth, eyes, head, and body. Less than a year earlier, their dreams of a young family had been shattered when they miscarried their first and only child. Now, with the drawn shades darkening her room, I imagined death inching closer, the Grim Reaper reaching his empty fingers toward her.

Yet when we sang prayerful songs over Emily, I lifted my eyes and saw an arresting sight. As Antonio held Emily's hand, his wedding ring glowed as if illuminated by an unseen, internal—or *eternal*—light. His fidelity lit up the darkness with gentle but unyielding force. Throughout our visit, the peace and resolve in Antonio's eyes were icons of hope in something still to come.

As he gently whispered to his bride, adjusted her bed, wiped her face, and blessed her broken body, he was faithfully loving her "to the dust."

Antonio shared with me how his fear of losing Emily had been steadily replaced by a resolve to give her the best he could, for however long he could. Antonio's ring of fidelity glowed stronger than death as it was forged in the fires of suffering. His life and Emily's truly had become one. The graces of the sacrament of marriage now held them united on the altar of fidelity, victoriously rising above despair to "present [their] bodies as a living sacrifice, holy and acceptable to God" (Rom 12:2).

So often we forget that the point of marriage is to lead a spouse into the communion from whence she or he originated. But how will that restoration occur? It won't be merely a spiritual journey; it will be bodily. As St. Paul notes, "For as by a man came death, by a man has come also the resurrection of the dead" (1 Cor 15:21).

Later, as I sat in my car with Antonio, he told me, "I think I know now that I am walking her into eternity." I quietly rejoiced as I saw God's love casting out the fear with which the Grim Reaper tried to grip Antonio. The October sun shone through the passenger window onto Antonio's wedding ring, blazing like the cry of St. Paul: "O death, where is your victory? O death, where is your sting?" (1 Cor 15:55). This same cry thundered forth from this bridegroom's faithful, enduring love of his bride, whose broken body will one day be fully restored.

Just 50 yards away the inflatable Grim Reaper flapped feebly in the breeze.

—⁓—

Reflect

Who am I afraid to lose to the reality of death? How can I focus on the resurrection that will occur after death, in the arms of the One who made us to walk with Him for eternity?

Challenge

Consider who in your life may be suffering illness or depression. Give them a call or visit today and encourage them to look beyond the grave to the hope of our final resurrection.

Pray

Lord, help me to be unafraid to confront death. Help me remember that, when embraced by your love, death is a gateway to eternal life. Amen.

16

Joyful Celibacy

by Joey Martineck

"You were made for the Kingdom."

- BRIDEGROOM

"I want to be with you," she said to him.

Stacy had finally worked up the courage to tell one of her best friends that she had feelings for him. Though sorority life had led her into some bad choices, Stacy experienced a major turnaround during college. Partially out of an attraction to this guy, she became increasingly more involved with the church and pro-life movement. But when her friend responded that he didn't feel the same way, she felt crushed.

St. Ignatius, the great spiritual advisor, spoke often to his directees about God leading us through the attractions of the heart. Stacy's desire for this romantic relationship and the subsequent disappointment was not just a meaningless, sad episode. The experience itself led her to realize that there is only one man who could ever wholly satisfy her heart: Jesus. Stacy's original attraction ultimately led her to discover her vocation as a religious sister with the Sisters of Life, a vocation that gives her deep joy and fulfillment.

Stacy's vocation and embrace of celibacy is often perplexing to a world that idolizes romantic love. Do you recall our discussion of how earthly marriage is a sign of the heavenly marriage of Christ and the Church? Heavenly marriage—union with God— is the ultimate destiny for every person. This is the reason that some people, like Stacy, are called to a life of celibacy for the Kingdom (cf. Matt 19:12). Celibacy is the decision for a man or woman to voluntarily forgo earthly marriage (and, therefore, sexual intimacy), thus witnessing "to the world that 'the kingdom of God is here'" and that heavenly marriage is real.[26]

Earthly marriage is a glorious gift to us from God. But it's not everything. Consider why Jesus indicates that there is no marriage in Heaven (cf. Luke 20:34-36). Signs help point us to a destination. In Heaven, the sign of marriage is no longer necessary because we have "arrived" at what marriage was pointing us toward all along: union with God Himself.

—∞—

Reflect

Am I open to a call to celibacy "for the sake of the Kingdom" as described in Matthew 19:12? If I am married, am I open to this vocation for my children? Why or why not?

Challenge

Visit a seminary or a convent. Ask questions to explore your own vocation or simply to better educate yourself.

Pray

Lord Jesus, I fear that a call to celibacy for me (or my children) means missing out on love, friendship, pleasure, and happiness. Change my mind and heart to see celibacy as a path to intimacy with God and others, fruitful in both this life and the next. Help me to be honest with what I truly desire for myself and my family and trust that you will my good. Amen.

17

The Disease

by Brian Butler

"One side effect I forgot to mention:
The Disease that has no cure!"

- SERPENT

I grew up in rural Louisiana where I interacted with nature often while hunting and fishing in the woods and creeks throughout my boyhood. We also faced dangerous encounters with venomous snakes or aggressive raccoons that frothed at the mouth with rabies infection. Most people would agree that, compared to venom and rabies, armadillos don't fit into the "dangerous" category. We usually encountered these nocturnal creatures at night as they dug holes and foraged around in our yard. Due to their poor eyesight, whenever we surprised them, the armadillos would hop in the air and sometimes dart right toward us. The sight of the bewildered creatures was hilarious, and I generally thought of armadillos as harmless until one night my Dad mentioned that we should never, ever touch them. His reason? Armadillos in Texas and Louisiana are carriers of a contagious disease known as leprosy.

Leprosy is a chronic infectious disease that incubates for years and progresses slowly over time. It causes serious skin lesions, and in severe cases, disfigurement and deformity. Leprosy is one of the oldest recorded human diseases, and in first century Palestine, leprosy had no known cure. Thus, in Jesus' day, lepers were outcasts and their prognosis was hopeless.

In Matthew's Gospel, we see Jesus' desire to heal the hopeless, including those afflicted with the devastating disease: "When Jesus came down from the mountain, great crowds followed him.

And then a leper approached, did him homage, and said, 'Lord, if you wish, you can make me clean.' He stretched out his hand, touched him, and said, 'I will do it. Be made clean.' His leprosy was cleansed immediately" (Mt 8:1–3).

Leprosy is rare today, and modern medicine has made it treatable. But even today, without treatment, advanced leprosy can cause paralysis and blindness. While we may not suffer *skin* disease, you and I do carry a *sin* disease that profoundly affects us every day. Original sin is an affliction of our humanity passed on to us from Adam and Eve. Though Baptism cleanses us of original sin, the effects of original sin still remain in the form of our *concupiscence.* Our own personal sin advances the "disease" and exacerbates its effects. Theologian Dr. Brant Pitre once taught me that sin makes us weak and stupid. Our inability to see things as they are is an effect of concupiscence. By darkening our intellects and weakening our wills, sin renders us like spiritual lepers: *spiritually paralyzed and unable to see.*

In the years I worked as a high school teacher, one of my students once radically defended his own blamelessness, saying, "I would not have chosen the fruit like Adam. I don't even *like* fruit!" But stopping here is taking the bait from the Enemy, continuing the blame-game that began in Eden. It's true that Adam and Eve passed on the disease of sin to us, but we must also recognize our responsibility for our own sins, for "all have sinned and are deprived of the glory of God" (Rom 3:23). And honestly, many of us have committed more than a few offenses against God, others, and ourselves by choosing selfishly and sinning abundantly.

So, you might ask yourself: Can I somehow escape concupiscence completely? Not in this life, but Jesus promises that the disease will be eradicated fully in His kingdom if we continue to open to Him along the way. The Good News is that our redemption progresses *now* as Christ transforms us daily, "For just as through the disobedience of one person the many were made sinners, so through the obedience of one the many will be made righteous . . . where sin increased, grace overflowed all the more" (Rom 5:19-20).

—m—

Reflect

Where in my life is my sin disease most prominent? When I look honestly at my life and choices, in what areas do I deny that I suffer the disease of sin? Where do I most need Jesus' love to cure me?

Challenge

Do an examination of conscience by meditating on the whole chapter of Romans 5. Locate where your sin has increased over the years, and where specifically you need to ask for an overflow of Christ's grace. If you are Catholic, complete this examination of conscience with a potent, known cure for sin: the Sacrament of Reconciliation.

Pray

Lord, I am not worthy of your love, but at your word, I believe you can heal me of my sin. Give me the courage to repent, believe in the Gospel, and live totally for you. Amen.

18

Hiding

by Joey Martineck

"Where are you?"

~ ADAM

One day when I was about 11, my dad told me to help him lift some boxes in the garage. When I got to the garage, there were no boxes. There was just Dad standing in the center of the empty area.

"Come here," he said.

I approached with hesitation. Dad looked at me without speaking for moment. Then he said he knew that I had starting looking at pornographic images on the computer.[27] His tone was calm but direct: "God does not want you to do that."

The air left my lungs. I had been caught red-handed. I felt physically weak and began to tremble, tears of shame running down my face. I just wanted to disappear from Dad's gaze.

But at that moment my dad leapt forward to embrace me in a powerful hug. I cried harder and harder, but he did not let go.

Like Adam and Eve experienced after the Fall, shame often compels us to hide ourselves from God and one another. Throughout my life, I've battled the urge to hide myself out of the fear that the real, raw me isn't good enough. I "hide" behind my accomplishments, hobbies, or what other people think. But these facades are just modern fig leaves, and authentic love sees through them.

God is never disgusted with the real, raw me or you. He knows every deep, hidden part of us and loves us unconditionally. He runs into our shame, inviting us to reveal ourselves fully before

Him and others who can uplift us. God's love frees us from having to hide behind masks.

Reflecting back now, this desire to be known and loved is what the 11-year-old me was really searching for on the computer. Words cannot describe how grateful I am to my dad for helping me root out what could have easily become a porn addiction. Dad's response of truth and unconditional love embodied the Father's heart to me. God doesn't want only a cleaned-up version of us. He wants us as real and raw as we are right now.

—⁓—

Reflect

Do I struggle with being duplicitous or fake?

Challenge #1

Next time you are with a trusted friend or group of friends, take the opportunity to be vulnerable and share truthfully whatever you have been carrying in your heart. Don't succumb to the temptation to tell others only what you think they want to hear.

Challenge #2

The band Casting Crowns' song "House of Their Dreams" articulates the interior hiding that often occurs in our relationships because of fear and shame. Listen to it prayerfully.

Pray

Lord Jesus, I am afraid to be honest with you and myself. Give me the grace to reveal myself fully to you, hiding nothing. Let me experience your love breaking through my shame. Amen.

19

Self Image

by Brian Butler

"A special polished stone to help you see how beautiful you look."
- SERPENT

Whether in our body shape, skin tone, eye color, or imperfectly ordered hair (or lack thereof), it's easy to find blemishes when we obsess in the mirror over attaining a perfect image. The "polished stones" offered by modern times only deepen this obsession. Even more than we do with mirrors, we stare constantly into screens that present, color, and edit our images before us. We point the lens back at ourselves in a search for *something*.

This "selfie" culture has real impact beyond the screen and pixels. In 2013, the Oxford Dictionary declared "selfie" to be the word of the year. Later, a study by the *Journal of Family Medicine* found that, over a span of a few years, 259 deaths worldwide were caused during or because of a selfie.[28] Never in the history of the world have we taken so many images of ourselves or shared so many of them with others. Endless editing and promotion of our selfies has led to unprecedented insecurity, shifting ideas of identity, ambiguous self-image . . . and even death.

While selfie-related physical death is tragic but relatively rare, the psychological and spiritual deaths are numerous. *Many people die in the concentration camps of comparison.* This deadly comparison comes not only in comparing ourselves to *others*, but also to broken images of ourselves.

In the beginning, surely Eve saw beauty when she first saw her own reflection on the surface of a quiet pool of water. Yet even more beautiful was the love she saw accompanying her reflection when she gazed into Adam's eyes. But today, when we find ourselves insecure, we often make the mistake of turning back to shallow affirmation instead of authentic self-gift. Our digital "friends" can offer only the quickly-evaporating emotional fix of a comment, proverbial "like," or "thumbs up."

Consider the modern scheme of endless, circular restlessness and self-preoccupation Satan has exploited. The temptation to find affirmation of our identity in the ever-shifting opinions of others follows us nearly 24–7. What's trending, beautiful, or fashionable changes daily. But what are we really looking for in our screens? Have we depersonalized ourselves through endless self-promotion rather than growing through self-gift? When we promote ourselves, we lose ourselves. When we truly give ourselves, we find the true identity we long for.

In a section of his writing called "Man in Search for His Essence," St. John Paul II notes that, though man is alone in Eden, he "finds himself from the first moment of his existence *before God* in search . . . of his own 'identity.'"[29] This is still true today. Where must we look to find ourselves? Not in the virtual eyes of others through our screens, but in the eyes of God: "Because you are precious in my eyes, and honored, and I love you" (Is 43:4).

—⁂—

Reflect

How might I be seeking affirmation from others in unhealthy and unfruitful ways? By seeking shallow affirmation instead of authentic self-gift, have I reduced others to a means to my own popularity, laughs, or good feelings?

Challenge

Commit to a true fast from social media one day this (or every) week. As you do so, offer up your fast for someone who needs to know he or she is loved by God.

Pray

Lord, help me to remember that you are constantly looking at me with delight. Please empower me to reject anything that offends my dignity as your child, and help me to stand up for the dignity of my brothers and sisters around me. Amen.

20

Forgiveness

by Joey Martineck

"I forgive you"
- EVE

In Lin-Manuel Miranda's outstanding musical *Hamilton*, title character Alexander has colossally damaged his marriage after years of infidelity and disordered priorities. After the tragic death of his son, Alexander begins to "spend hours in the garden," reflecting on his mistakes. He attempts to reconcile with his wife, Eliza, knowing she has no reason to take him back.

The lyrics of the song "It's Quiet Uptown" progress as follows:

> *There are moments that the words don't reach,*
> *There is grace too powerful to name,*
> *We push away what we can never understand,*
> *We push away the unimaginable.*
> *They are standing in the garden,*
> *Alexander by Eliza's side,*
> *She takes his hand,*
> *It's quiet uptown.*

Then the Company comes in strong:

> *Forgiveness. Can you imagine?*
> *Forgiveness. Can you imagine?*

Eliza shows her husband completely undeserved mercy. Jesus, too, has mercy to offer us and is actually eager to do so (cf. Luke

22:15). He does not merely forgive us from a distance—He wants us to know that we have been forgiven and that we belong to Him. Mercy is a defining characteristic of God's love. St. John Paul II put it this way: "We are not the sum of our weaknesses and failures; we are the sum of the Father's love for us and our real capacity to become the image of his Son."[30]

Forgiveness toward others is not optional for Christians. Jesus Himself taught us to pray, "Forgive us our trespasses as we forgive those who trespass against us" (Matt 6:12). This doesn't mean God will withhold forgiveness from us if we fail to forgive others perfectly. Rather, if we don't strive to offer forgiveness, we won't be fully able to receive the forgiveness God has for us.

It's often the hardest to forgive ourselves. One day in college I went to confession with the campus priest, Fr. Tim Hepburn. I was being really hard on myself for what I had done. After I had confessed my sins, Fr. Tim looked at me and said, "Joey, do you know that when God the Father looks at you, He sees His beloved son, with whom He is well pleased?" (cf. Matt 3:17). He gave me absolution and then, choked up, I said, "Thank you." I went to the chapel and cried my eyes out. It was the first time I had become truly aware of God's love for me as a son.

—◊◊◊—

Reflect

How do I imagine the Father sees me as I stand before Him?

Challenge

Forgive someone. Ask the Lord to bring to mind someone you need to forgive, even if it's yourself. If it's helpful, imagine a courtroom and the judge whacking the mallet down saying "_____ is hereby acquitted of all charges in the court of law."

Pray

Lord Jesus, you asked your Father to forgive the ones who nailed you to the cross. Help us to believe that we share in your Sonship and that you will never stop fighting for us to receive your forgiveness. Amen.

21

Seeing the Good

by Brian Butler

"What is there to like about my ears?"

- ADAM

When I was a kid, I had big ears. Nothing was medically "wrong" with them, but they seemed different than everyone else's ears. Later on, this feeling deepened when I sustained a wound to one of my ears that rendered it permanently different than the other one. After blood, anger, and long looks in the mirror, I felt like my imbalanced ear was the only thing others saw when they looked at me. Not my smile, not my eyes. All they saw was my ear, protruding off the side of my head.

The Enemy's mockery of the good body God had given me amplified when kids teased me and called me names. These wounds spawned a lie that I came to believe as absolute truth about my body: *I had a 'bad side.'* For years whenever I posed for a photo, I would cock my head to show only my *good side* to the camera, and to hide the *bad side.* It took years for God to heal that wound in my heart.

Our goodness—body and soul—is literally on page one of our story in the Bible: "God created man in his own image . . . male and female he created them . . . And God saw [what] he had made, and behold, it was very good" (Gen 1:27, 31). How, then, do we explain physical brokenness and imperfection? The writings of St. Thomas Aquinas helped me understand that there *is* plenty of brokenness in the world, but defects, disorder, and human death are all the effects of original sin. None of these change or diminish the truth of our inherent goodness.

So often we focus on what is imperfect, broken, or lacking in our bodies, blinding us to what is so very, very good. My constant preoccupation with my "bad side" drove me to compensate by covering it with my "good side." This took the form of overachieving, an imbalanced view of winning in athletics, and attempting to build my self-worth through *doing what I thought would look good* in the eyes of others.

Yet the truth is that when considering the *essence* of who we are, *we do not have a bad side.* Despite being wounded by physical and moral evils in the world, including our own sin, we find the truth of our identity and our goodness in God's gaze. His gaze upon us reveals the truth of our worth.

In a letter about the Sabbath, the Lord's day, St. John Paul II wrote about how God looks at us:

> "The divine rest of the seventh day does not allude to an inactive God, but emphasizes the fullness of what has been accomplished. It speaks, as it were, of God's lingering before the 'very good' work (Gen 1:31) which his hand has wrought, in order to cast upon it *a gaze full of joyous delight.* This is a 'contemplative' gaze, which does not look to new accomplishments but enjoys the beauty of what has already been achieved. It is a gaze which God casts upon all things, but in a special way upon man, the crown of creation."[31]

Since our first moment of existence, He has gazed upon us with "joyous delight." Our value doesn't come after the fact from "new accomplishments" or how we view ourselves in the mirror of our minds, but comes from our very being. Is this the way we look upon—and value—ourselves and all those around us?

—∞—

Reflect

Have I allowed what I think about my body (looks, weight, hairstyle, etc) to change what I believe about myself, my core identity? What truth does God want to reveal about how He sees me and looks upon me?

Challenge

Consider the truth of how God made you very good, unique, and differ-ent than others. Ask someone you trust to look you in the eye and affirm the good they see in you. Later, in your heart, ask God this bold question: How did I reflect your great beauty today, Lord?

Pray

Lord, help me to see myself not merely as a collection of parts in the mir-ror, but as the whole, good, beautiful person you made me to be. Help me gain a new routine rooted in the truth of your love when I look in the mirror. Amen.

22

Counterfeit and Fullness

by Aimee MacIver

"You never used to look at me that way before."

- EVE

When I was a little girl, I spent most of my time running barefoot around gravel roads and traipsing through the woods. Most of my outfits ended up streaked with the dust and grime of a day outdoors. But occasionally, a special event called for dressing up. I reveled in these special details: dresses made of lace, shiny patent leather shoes, knotted braids traded for fancy curls.

Often when I had buttoned the last button and smoothed the last wisp, I presented myself to my dad for the affirmation I knew he would offer and which I deeply desired. "Wow!" he'd say. "You are so beautiful!" His words filled me with peace and a sense of freedom. Because I trusted his love, I believed his words. I knew he didn't mean only that the way I looked was beautiful—he meant that I *myself* was beautiful! This belief lifted my heart and made me feel seen and whole.

Eventually, childhood gave way to adolescence, and the inevitable hurts and disappointments of life accumulated into mounting insecurity. I began to read teen magazines loaded with contradictory and confusing messages: *Looks aren't everything. But here are 25 ways to be prettier and skinnier by spring break.* Advertising and peer pressure only deepened my awareness of my own inadequacy in meeting impossible, ever-shifting beauty standards. My appearance became a source of anxiety.

One day at a social gathering, as I nervously hoped my outfit and my hair looked okay, a guy very openly stopped to look me up and down in a way that I had never experienced before. "Girl," he said, not using my name, "you look hot."

Struck as though by a thunderbolt, I realized that my appearance had power. I could use it to gain attention that, for a moment, relieved my insecurity. Attractiveness could be a kind of currency. I could use it to "buy" what seemed like the only thing for sale: the brief flare of hope that if I could grasp notice, maybe eventually someone would look long enough to see *me*. It took years and the healing of many wounds to see clearly that the entire exchange was a counterfeit. Superficial attention can never satisfy because it reduces the value of the entire person into only one dimension. And when value depends solely upon appearance, it is as fleeting and fickle as magazine trends.

As women, we sometimes tragically suffer the unwanted objectification of men indulging their lust. But the counterfeit of authentic affirmation has seduced many women into *objectifying themselves* by using their own bodies as a currency, not honoring beauty as a revelation of the infinitely beautiful person but wielding it as a weapon of manipulation, competition, and domination.

In the beginning, Adam delighted in beholding Eve's physical beauty that signaled the beauty of her whole person. But as it does with other goods, sin distorts and inverts the meaning and power of beauty. Physical beauty is a gift meant to reveal the breathtaking beauty of the human person; concupiscence attempts to isolate physical attractiveness as the only good considered, and results in concealing the person's true dignity under false conditions.

Our hope lies in being filled again with the Father's love, and refusing to empty ourselves over and over for a counterfeit. The woman who received God's love most perfectly shows us how. When we call Mary "full of grace," we should contemplate that word—*full*. Her womanhood and identity is wholly filled by her trust in the Father's love, by her belief in His goodness. And in her fullness, Mary is free.

—⁓—

Reflect

When have I experienced the counterfeit of authentic affirmation? When I experienced the fullness of love? How are the counterfeit and fullness of love different in their effects?

Challenge #1

When you look in the mirror, try an exercise of affirmation with yourself. For example, look at your eyes: how beautiful they are because of what they allow you to receive and share! When you feel insecurities rising about your appearance, make an intentional gesture of gratitude for your body. For example, thank God for the way your body allows you to receive and give love.

Challenge #2

Think of someone you struggle to see rightly and prepare to see them anew: View them as God would, avoiding lust or comparison. Look beyond their physical appearance. Look in their eyes. Look at them through the lens of their true dignity and focus on the gift that they are.

Pray

Lord, I am wondrously made in your image. Fill me with trust in your love. Free me from the false idol of seeking physical perfection. Fill any insecurity with your grace. Mother Mary, pray for me to receive God wholly so that I, too, may be made whole. Amen.

23

Looking

by Joey Martineck

"Do you like it when I look at you this way?"

- ADAM

I began trying to take purity seriously in college. My first strategy was to avert my eyes whenever I felt a strong physical attraction to a woman's appearance. If I didn't look, I couldn't lust, right? After walking around with my head down for basically a whole month, I began to question if this wary approach was really a mature expression of purity.

Discouraged, I asked my longtime friend and spiritual director, Fr. Tim Hepburn, for guidance. He said, "What if the next time you experience a lustful temptation, you command it to stand before the feet of Jesus and be judged by Him?"

The truth is: purity isn't primarily something that *we* do. Practicing purity does indeed take intention and effort on our part, but our effort must flow from inviting God to do the hard labor of transforming our hearts.

Remember that our bodies are "very good" (Gen 1:31). It's not that our bodies (including our sex drive) suddenly became bad after the Fall. Rather, our way of seeing the body became wounded. Before the Fall, Adam beheld Eve's body and saw immediately God's image and her immeasurable dignity, but sin distorted the lens.

Jesus' words about this topic sound harsh at first: "You have heard that it was said 'You shall not commit adultery'. But I say to you, everyone who looks at a woman with lust has already committed adultery with her in his heart" (Matt 5:27–28). Yikes! Yet in response to this Gospel passage, St. John Paul II asks: "Should we fear the severity of Christ's words, or have confidence in their salvific content, in their power to save?"[32]

St. John Paul II dared to believe that Christ offers us real power to overcome lust and every disordered desire. This is not just the power of forgiveness after a fall. This is not a power that we muster up by ourselves. This is a power that flows from the heart of Christ which can be realized in our bodies if we are open to it. This is a power that actually changes our *hearts*.

"Turn away your eyes" (Sir 9:8, RSV-CE) is good advice for someone on the first steps toward purity. After all, Christ says, "If your eye causes you to sin, pluck it out" (Mk 9:47). We should not take risks when it comes to sin. However, our journey cannot end there. Christ did not come simply to give us coping mechanisms to help us avoid sin; He came to redeem us![33] He offers us *new* eyes to see the glory of God in the human body. Rather than turning away from beauty like I did for so long, God is inviting you and me—through a path of redemption not exempt from suffering—to a more pure, more mature way of looking at man and woman that raises us in awe of Beauty Himself.

—⁓—

Reflect

Am I living in Christian freedom that comes from virtue? Or are my efforts toward purity just coping mechanisms?

Challenge

Take time to meditate on Catholic art that depicts the nude human body. When artists display human nakedness in order to arouse lust, the result is pornography. But true sacred art showing the body's goodness and beauty is intended to raise our hearts and minds to God's glory.

Pray

Lord Jesus, help me to see the human body as you created it to be seen— the visible presence of another human person made wondrously in your image. Amen.

24

Battlefield of the Heart

by Brian Butler

"Tonight, you will join your body with Eve's."

- BRIDEGROOM

As Adam first looked upon Eve with pure wonder and joy, he exclaimed, "This one, at last, is bone of my bones and flesh of my flesh" (Gen 2:23). When God gave Adam and Eve to one another, their movement from solitude into union was defined by reverence for God's plan and design. The permanent and unbreakable unity between the first man and the first woman was the first marriage—a union established by God.

Scripture records that after God gave them to each other, He gave them His first command for the proper embrace of sex: "Be fruitful and multiply" (Gen 1:28). From the beginning, God designed sex to be a fruitful gift—a life-giving act. In the sexual act, husband and wife give the gift of themselves to each other through the mutual gift of their bodies. According to God's design, sex doesn't just belong in marriage as if marriage is a mere moral boundary. Rather, sex is marital by its very nature; sex makes visible the true nature of marriage.

But living the gift of our sexuality according God's design has been a key battle for man and woman *almost* from the beginning. Approaching sexual intimacy with trust and obedience to God's plan today, and ordering our sexual desires toward authentic love can seem impossible sometimes.

After reserving sex for marriage throughout high school and college, and then dating Lisa for more than four years, I felt Adam's words leap into my own heart as our wedding day approached: *"At last!"* Yet, even as deeply as I loved Lisa, I recognized my heart still struggled to love purely. I had not yet encountered St. John Paul II's beautiful insights on marriage and sexuality, but I already sensed that I had a clear choice to make. I could allow my sexual desires to master me and dominate my wife, or I could master my sexual desires and order them toward love (cf. Gen 3:16).[34] If lust engages our sexual desire *apart* from God's love and design, then love fulfills sexual desire *according* to God's love and His plans. I loved Lisa far too much to allow my weaknesses and lust to reign. As we approached our honeymoon, I resolved to intentionally place our union in the hands of God and turned to Scripture.

The Old Testament book of Tobit tells the story of a demon that had killed seven consecutive husbands on their wedding night with the same woman, Sarah. Instead of running away from this dark history, Tobias chooses to confront the demon and takes Sarah to be his wife. On their wedding night, Tobias prays, "And now, O Lord, I am not taking this sister of mine because of lust, but with sincerity. Grant that I may find mercy and grow old together with her" (Tob 8:7) God answers Tobias' prayer by granting the couple life. In analyzing the lessons of Tobias and Sarah's story, St. John Paul II notes, "from the very first moment, Tobias' love has *to face the test of life-or-death.* Tobias (and Sarah with him) go without hesitating toward this test. Life has the victory [because] during the test of the wedding night, love is revealed as stronger than death."[35]

I wanted God's love to triumph in my heart and in our marriage. So on our wedding night, Lisa and I prayed the prayer of Tobias and Sarah, consecrating our bodily union to God's love. Over the course of our marriage, our choice to surrender to God's design has not always been easy, and at times has entailed some long and painful struggles. Choosing to trust Christ and His Church means agreeing to give ourselves to each other freely, faithfully, and *totally*—holding back nothing from each other, not even our fertility. Many regard the Church's teaching on contraception as radical, and the faithful practice of natural family planning as burdensome. But for Lisa and I, fully embracing God's intended design has been beautiful beyond imagination!

Mutually free, faithful, and total self-gift has become a cornerstone of our marriage, and has made it fruitful spiritually, emotionally, and physically. The security of our marriage has largely come from the commitment to reverence—a gift of the Holy Spirit. The Holy Spirit cultivates "in man and woman . . . reverence for the two inseparable meanings of the conjugal act."[36] Reverence never rushes or controls the gift, but safeguards these two meanings: "the unitive significance and the procreative significance which are both inherent to the marriage act."[37] By safeguarding these essential aspects of sex, spouses protect each other and their union, ensuring that it remains an act of love. Contraception, by its very nature, separates union and procreation and therefore undermines the very meaning and purpose of sexuality. The Church prohibits contraception not because she devalues sex, but because she upholds its dignity and power to express God's love.

Praying for the grace to approach God, each other, and the gift of our sexuality with reverence is the secret to victorious love. Only by God's power can we engage our sexuality with real freedom, totality, faithfulness, and fruitfulness, which in turn images His love. Only by trusting His design can we triumph on the "battlefield between love and concupiscence"[38] in our hearts and the whole of our lives.

—⁓⁓—

Reflect

Which Church teachings on sexuality and marriage do I struggle with? How can I go deeper into these teachings in order to resolve my struggle?

Challenge

Prayerfully read St. Paul VI's encyclical Humanae Vitae, which is available online at www.vatican.va. Research Natural Family Planning methods with an open mind, leaving aside any preconceived ideas or skepticism.[39] Many parishes and other apostolates offer classes in

NFP instruction; consider taking one to learn more about the beauty of embracing God's design for sexuality.

Pray

Holy Spirit, initiate a deeper reverence in me for the gift of my body and my fertility. May that reverence translate into deeper appreciation for the powers of life and love you have placed within me. Amen.

25

Grasping

by Joey Martineck

*"I was reaching 'cause nothing else in front
of me could ease the hurt."*

- ADAM

One Christmas, my grandparents decided to spend the holiday in Florida with some friends. A couple of weeks before, they dropped off their gifts at our house along with clear instructions that the packages were not to be opened until Christmas Day.

Later on, with no one around to see, I convinced my little brother to open one of the gifts. In a matter of minutes, shredded wrapping paper littered the floor under the tree and every last gift was opened. When our parents finally came into the room, they were furious.

Discipline followed. On Christmas Day, our parents made us wait thirty minutes after waking up to open Santa's presents: absolute torture for excited little kids. Our parents and grandparents wanted to give us the gifts under the Christmas tree. But they wanted to give them to us on the best terms, terms they understood more deeply and wisely than we did.

In Genesis, the fruit of the Tree of Knowledge of Good and Evil is described as "pleasing to the eyes and desirable" (Gen 3:6). What if the problem with Adam and Eve eating the fruit is not so much the fruit itself or the eating itself? What if the real problem was that instead of receiving the fruit, they grasped for it?

We often find this same "grasping" in our relationships. St. John Paul II describes how after the Fall, the dynamic between man and woman shifts from a relationship of gift "into a relationship of appropriation."[40] Where Eve once gave herself freely to Adam, she now is tempted to manipulate him. Where Adam once gave himself freely to Eve, he now is tempted to objectify and possess her. Both are tempted to grasp instead of patiently receive; their understanding of the gift becomes distorted. We must constantly invite Christ into this inclination to grasp, the tug toward sin called concupiscence, so that He can redeem our desires and give us trust in the Father.

—∞—

Reflect

What gift am I grasping for in my life right now that I doubt God will provide?

Challenge

Journal about some specific things for which you are longing. Concretely ask God to grant them to you. Later you can look back on this and thank God for the ways He has been faithful.

Pray

Lord Jesus Christ, my heart is filled with desires. I open them up before you without hiding anything. I trust in your goodness that you will fulfill them in your perfect time. Amen.

26

Closed Hearts

by Brian Butler

*"Run and hide / I'm starting to believe you're /
not worth the fight."*

- ADAM & EVE

One night when Lisa and I were dating, we had a serious fight as I was driving her home. When we arrived at her house, neither of us wanted to leave, but neither was able to apologize. We stayed in the car, in silence, for almost an hour. It was excruciating as we both wondered what the other was thinking. As the silence grew darker, I was torn between reasonable questions, unfair accusations, deep seated fears, hopes for peace, real anger, growing insecurity, and crumbling trust.

In St. John Paul II's reflections on Genesis, he notes that "shame . . . replaced absolute trust connected with the earlier state of original innocence."[41] When God first placed Adam and Eve in the Garden, their "original innocence" was a complete purity of heart that allowed them to mutually see each other and interact with authentic love. This purely selfless love created a secure relationship in which they had the "peace of the interior gaze" that creates true intimacy.[42] If I had known these truths back then, I would likely have been even more upset about how far from them we were that night.

As we navigate relational obstacles in friendship, dating, and marriage, it's important to learn from our mistakes. But it's key that we learn the *right thing* from them in order to move forward after our "falls."

With nearly 900 million views (as of December 2018) of her music video, "Wide Awake," consider the lyrics of Katy Perry's famous song:

Falling from cloud nine / Crashing from the high
I'm letting go tonight / I'm falling from cloud nine
I'm wide awake / Not losing any sleep
Picked up every piece / And landed on my feet
I'm wide awake / Need nothing to complete myself, no

In human experience, there can be a fine line between justified, prudent self-protection and an unhealthy, closed-off self-reliance. In fact, even experiencing shame can be healthy and fruitful if it "indicates the threat to the value, and at the same time it preserves this value in an interior way."[43] For example, when the royal garden of a woman's heart, mind, and body has been violated, manipulated, or used, her natural desire may be to close or conceal the garden. This instinct actually springs from recognizing the value of the woman and attempting to preserve it. Woman or man, we all have this interior movement toward self-defense when our dignity is violated. When someone hurts us, we have right reason to guard our hearts even more closely than before, because our hearts are indeed precious and worthy of protection.

But prudent protection is *not* the same as *hardening* our hearts, running away, and receding into ourselves. When we reflect upon our mistakes and wounds in order to learn from them, we must not let fear dominate our lives and responses. If we do, our experience of differences can become toxic. This "toxic" type of shame can trap us behind walls of self-reliance that block out love. But God is far more capable of protecting and healing than we are of hurting or being hurt.

Without intentional reflection, it's easy to develop a habit of rigid self-defense and live in fear of the past, rather than seeking healing and learning to trust again in freedom. No one can deny that woundedness makes self-gift tough and self-reliance tempting. But St. John Paul II encourages us, "Does this mean that we should distrust the human heart? No! It is only to say that we must remain in control of it."[44]

When we are hurt through relational "falls," Christ invites us to entrust ourselves completely to Him, asking to be wide awake and open to future relationships by balancing prudent self-protection with the power of self-gift.

—⚬—

Relect

Have I reacted to hurts from the opposite sex by attempting to devalue men or women all together? What walls of self-defense need to slowly come down in my own heart and life?

Challenge

This week, stretch yourself in an area where you rely too much on yourself. When someone asks if you need help, accept the service. When you feel overwhelmed or stressed, ask a friend for help. Reach out if you feel lonely and need community, or ask forgiveness from someone you know you have hurt because of your own self-reliance.

Pray

Holy Spirit, keep me wide awake to reverence the gift of myself and of others. Help me to open again to receive healing in the places I have been hurt, and help me to learn to protect my dignity and the dignity of those around me. Amen.

27

Casting Doubt

by Joey Martineck

"You're a greedy miser."

- SERPENT

In *Harry Potter and the Prisoner of Azkaban*, the wizarding world lives in terror of escaped convict Sirius Black, a murderer with dark, selfish motives. Sirius is actually Harry's godfather, but even Harry fears and avoids the wizard because of his infamous reputation.

Spoiler alert: When Harry finally meets Sirius Black for the first time personally, he learns the truth. Sirius is actually a good man who has been framed by a deceiver for his supposed crimes. All along, even as Harry feared and hid from his godfather, Sirius wished only to pour his protection and love over his godson.

What image do you have of God the Father? Leading up to the Fall, the *Catechism of the Catholic Church* describes how Adam and Eve "became afraid of the God of whom they have conceived a distorted image."[45] When they encounter the Serpent in the Garden, Satan paints a picture of God that casts doubt upon His good nature. Satan's lie is simple but profoundly effective: *You think God is good? Ha! He's nothing but a tyrant. He tells you only what gives him control. He couldn't care less about your best interests.*[46] Adam and Eve fall for this lie and "let their trust in their Creator die in their hearts."[47]

Our own sins often reenact the original Fall. When you and I knowingly choose to sin, our disobedience usually flows from a lack of trust in God's goodness and from the fear that springs from a distorted image of God. The Serpent preys upon Adam and Eve's fear with the lie that if they eat the fruit, they "will be like God"

(Gen 3:5 RSV-CE). The lie distorts an actual truth: in fact, from the moment of their creation, man and woman are "destined to be fully divinized by God in glory."[48] But rather than trusting God to bring their desires to fulfillment, Adam and Eve succumb to fear that God isn't good and take matters into their own hands.

My scripture professor, Dr. Gregory Vall, once explained that ever since the first sin cast doubt upon God's good nature, God's main response has been to reveal Himself. Oh what wonder! The history of Israel, the prophets, and ultimately the mystery of Jesus' Incarnation, Passion and Resurrection: these are God's patient attempts to correct the distorted image we have conceived of Him.

—⁂—

Reflect

In what ways might my image of God be distorted by fear or lies?

Challenge

Spend time journaling to dialogue with God. Directly address any specific ways you feel God is holding out on you and communicate this to Him. Finally, give God space to respond.

Pray

Lord, we mistook you for a tyrant, yet for our sake, tyrants put you to death. We feared you were holding us back, yet you allowed your hands to be nailed to the Cross. We doubted that you had our best interests at heart, yet your blood has made us new. Lord Jesus, thank you for revealing the Father to us. Help us always to trust and believe in your goodness. Amen.

28

Hurt and Glory

by Brian Butler

"He will hurt her . . . She will manipulate him.
The cycle will go on and on."

~ SERPENT

My wife, Lisa, was raised in a nominally-Jewish, nominally-Catholic home. Without a cohesive vision for faith and relationships, she often faced confusion on questions about love and sexuality. As she began dating, she proceeded without a guiding light towards true love. Exploring her desires for love led to an indulgent lifestyle and a hopelessness that led her to wonder where or even if God should be in the process at all.

Meanwhile, I was raised in a faithfully Catholic home, yet I attended a high school that favored following laws over cultivating virtue when it came to sexuality. I received rules for sexual morality without any reasons, which left a negative and repressive understanding of sexuality. For years, I hid my fears and disordered sexual fantasies in my heart. Rather than choosing indulgence, I repressed my sexuality, pretending my sexual desire didn't exist. But merely stuffing desires away meant I never learned how to cultivate the gift of sexuality. I didn't know how to master the fire of sexual desire because I mistakenly believed that chastity demanded only that I extinguish those flames.

One night, reaping the hurt of using and being used, Lisa looked in the mirror as despair filled her heart. Then, for the first time in her life, she heard God's voice: "Go to church." The next day at the restaurant where we both worked, she asked if anyone would go to church with her. I took one look at my cute coworker and easily made one of the best decisions of my life.

As our church visit grew into dating, I saw the effects that Lisa's former boyfriends had on her heart. She was open on the outside but locked up on the inside. Even now many years later and very happily married, God's mercy is still working out the kinks in her heart and mine. It is still not always easy for Lisa to be open, to let me in, or to give me all of herself. Why? She has tasted the pain of hurt and manipulation. And, sorrowfully, I haven't always perfectly respected her either, approaching her with reverence and purity. Why? All those years, I had thought that ignoring or burying lust would eliminate it. The great mistake was thinking that if only my lust was hidden deeply enough, then it wouldn't hurt anyone, or need to be examined by my conscience, or confessed, or redeemed by Jesus Christ.

The different wounds Lisa and I sustained on our journeys sometimes collide into a giant wedge, threatening to divide us from each other and the God who gave us to one another. The reality is that the Enemy still sneaks into the garden of our hearts, planting seeds of doubt. After our own personal falls, or being wounded by others, our tendency is to revert to the wound of Eden, withdrawing into ourselves and hiding from intimacy (cf Gen 3:8–10). Love always involves risk, but as members of the human family bearing wounds of the Fall, we struggle to take that risk.

Knowing this, St. John Paul II still repeated the call of the Second Vatican Council countless times: "Man cannot fully find himself except through a sincere gift of himself."[49] Notice the call is not to give a *perfect* gift of self, but a *sincere* gift of self. But if we open our wounds to God, He can and will transform them into glorious mysteries of resurrected love.

Thankfully, Lisa and I reap the rich rewards of entrusting our pasts, as well as our present, to the Lord's merciful healing. He has *never* let us down. The deeper we let Him enter our wounds and pray about them together, the more powerful His victory becomes in our lives! Day by day, we become more free. God's healing power has made a beautiful triumph: two indulgent, repressive sinners have repented, been forgiven, and are set free to explore such hopeful love!

—⚭—

Reflect

What physical, emotional, relational, and spiritual wounds have I sustained in my life regarding the gift of my own sexuality? How do the similar wounds of my spouse, family, or others in my life affect my relationship with them? Have I lost hope that Christ can redeem my past or the past of those I love? (Consider making a small retreat to reflect on these questions.)

Challenge

Reflect on your sexual formation and formative relationships in your past. Take the lid off your heart and offer God every single shred of darkness, confusion or hurt that is there. If you are married or seriously dating, discuss how your respective stories have shaped your relationship. Begin praying together daily specifically for each other's healing and freedom.

Pray

Lord Jesus, I offer you my past, my present, and my future. I invite you to enter the deepest places of hurt in my sexuality. Let my wounds be healed and become the places of your glory. Amen.

29

Woundedness

by Joey Martineck

"This is not how we were supposed to be."

- EVE

I will never forget the day I first met my beloved goddaughter, Allison. My friends had invited me over to meet their new daughter, who was healthy except for some complications to her hip. Had her doctor not caught the issue quickly, Allison would have grown up unable to walk properly.

As I looked for the first time upon this beautiful baby girl, lying with a tiny hip brace in her crib, I was rendered speechless. She was broken . . . I couldn't help but love her. Of course I wanted her to be healthy and able to walk. But in that moment, I didn't love her in spite of her being broken. Her condition actually moved my heart and stirred up my love more.

What if God the Father looks upon us the same way? What if instead of being repulsed by our brokenness, He draws closer to us? Some Christians believe that human nature was entirely corrupted by Adam and Eve's sin, and that Christ merely covers and masks our corruption like a blanket. What's the problem with this understanding of salvation? At the end of the day, we're just covered up, not healed, transformed, or made whole.

The *Catechism* affirms that even though the sin of our first parents caused devastating consequences, "human nature has not been totally corrupted."[50] This means that instead of thinking of ourselves as "rotten to the core" (as the movie *Descendants* puts it), we ought to see ourselves as wounded, while our intrinsic dignity remains.

Like Allison, we are born wounded. She bore a bodily suffering that was not her fault; we bear a wound in our souls passed on through the Fall of our first parents: concupiscence (the inclination to sin). In *GARDEN*, this is referred to as "The Disease." Many things we think of as "natural" to human experience are products of our inherited woundedness. For example, selfishness in a relationship is actually not natural to the way God originally designed us. The true vision of what it means to be human can be understood only in light of our creation as man and woman before the Fall along with the revelation of Jesus Christ.

But even though we may be wounded by sin, our brokenness is not an obstacle to God's love. God is never repulsed by our sinfulness. His love does not merely cover up and hide our misery so as to make us appear whole. If we allow Him to love us, God can actually transform us from the inside out.

—⁂—

Reflect

How am I wounded by sin? In what ways have I experienced God drawing closer to me in my brokenness?

Challenge

Be on the lookout for people who seem to be suffering from woundedness. When you notice them, instead of trying to "fix it," simply find a way to love them in their brokenness. Sometimes all this takes is simple affirmation or a listening ear.

Pray

Lord Jesus, you made me good. I allow you to love me in all the ways I am wounded and hurting. Amen.

30

Who Leads?

by Brian Butler

*"The dogs are barking as the distant thunder rolls /
neither of us has ever really been in control."*

- ADAM & EVE

Our dog, Max, is not a disciplined dog. An Australian Shepherd, his energy far outpaces mine, especially on cold winter mornings at 5:45 a.m. when I head out to jog. Max breaks into such a frenzy of excitement when he sees me pick up his leash that I have to wrestle him to get it on. Then the wild ride begins with a peculiar habit he repeats time and again. Max turns to face me, grabs the leash in his teeth, and spins away, racing to *lead me* where he wants to go. Though our tugs-of-war and sprints can be entertaining and enjoyable, sometimes he wears on my patience. But more than once, God has taught me deep truths through my relationship with Max.

In my prayer time with God, I'm a bit like Max with his master. I'm excited that God is with me, but overzealous to get moving. I struggle to slow down, pay attention, trust, listen, and follow. Like Max, I am more interested in tackling the world ahead than receiving the One who is daily leading me into that world. Why? I tend to act as a human *doing* rather than a human *being*. I would rather race down my *to-do* list than sit still with my *to-be* list. But this renders our perception of God into merely a guide or a master.

Prayer is not a check-in where we just tell God hello, get instructions or guidance, ask for things we need, or even get affirmed for doing something good. Prayer is a day-by-day, moment-by-moment invitation to fall deeper in love with God.

We do follow, but this following is not so much an act of doing. It's intentionally *being* in relationship. As we allow the Holy Spirit to lead us, He helps us let go of control and move to the deeper places we could never reach if we were the ones "leading."

St. John Paul II taught that "prayer develops that conversation with Christ which makes us his intimate friends: 'Abide in me and I in you' (Jn 15:4)."[51] It is not ultimately about duty but about intimacy, about becoming one with the God who made us for Himself. St. John Paul II goes on to explain that prayer can draw us deeper into love and, even through trials of life, finally to the joy of union with Jesus:

> ". . . prayer can progress, as a genuine dialogue of love, to the point of rendering the person wholly possessed by the divine Beloved, vibrating at the Spirit's touch, resting filially within the Father's heart. This is the lived experience of Christ's promise: 'He who loves me will be loved by my Father, and I will love him and manifest myself to him' (Jn 14:21). It is a journey totally sustained by grace, which nonetheless demands an intense spiritual commitment and is no stranger to painful purifications (the 'dark night'). But it leads, in various possible ways, to the ineffable joy experienced by the mystics as nuptial union."[52]

Vibrating at the Spirit's touch and resting in the Father's heart? That sounds like an intimacy born of *sensitivity.* Sensitivity grows from truly and intentionally listening. Listening follows from obedience to the One we trust. Heartfelt trust comes from personal knowledge of the One's trustworthiness. Personal knowledge develops from experience. To be an authentic learner is to be a *disciple* of someone who teaches and leads. And to be a disciple of Jesus is to learn from Him how to be human beings: how to let go of control and allow Him to *lead us* to everlasting life.

—◦◦◦—

Reflect

Where in my life am I trying to stay in control?

Challenge

When a would-be follower of Jesus declares, "I will follow you wherever you go," Jesus' reply is unexpectedly challenging. Read Luke 9:57–62 slowly and ask the Holy Spirit to reveal your excuses for not radically following Jesus. Then take a walk (with your dog, if you have one) and reflect on allowing the Lord to lead you. Ask God: Will you show me how to "relinquish the leash" and let you lead me in this area?

Pray

Lord Jesus, teach me to pray. In prayer, teach me to trust you and to follow you in obedience that draws me deeper into the joy of deep, intimate friendship as your true disciple. Amen.

31

Communion of Saints

by Joey Martineck

"My heart wants something bigger"

- EVE

Going back to Georgia Tech hurts. That's the best way I can describe it. When I go to visit the Catholic Center, I'm reminded of the karaoke nights, Friday night dinners, and evenings of praise and worship that have long passed. I'm reminded of the brotherhood in my men's group and of people I love who are no longer in my life. Sometimes I even find myself avoiding the place where I once felt totally accepted because I'm still grieving the loss of that community.

These aches of loss and absence are painful but can be highly instructive. They teach us that we are not supposed to be separated from the community where we love and are loved. We've been focusing on Heaven as the place of our ultimate union with God and the perfect restoration of our bodies. But Heaven is not only perfect union with God; Heaven is also perfect communion with one another. Heaven is community! The Church calls this "the communion of saints."

We shouldn't dismiss heavenly community as merely "pious sentiment." Imagine seeing, accepting, and caring for every person you have ever loved (with every conflict in those relationships resolved), and having this perfectly reciprocated to you, for all eternity. What an inconceivable joy! To me, I'm willing to sacrifice anything to obtain that "pearl of great price" (Matt 13:46).

St. John Paul II says that the Resurrection "will above all be man's rediscovery of himself, not only in the depths of his own person, but also in that union that is proper to the world of persons."[53] The Resurrection fulfills everything that we are made for, including relationships with others. If original solitude finds fulfilment in communion with God, the original unity of Adam and Eve finds fulfillment in the communion of saints. This communion is the "wedding feast" that the Scriptures prophesy and Jesus speaks of often (Rev 19:9; Matt 22:1–14). All are invited, and no one is excluded!

Contrasted with this glorious vision, the type of "free love" the world heralds is really an impoverished version of the love we're made for. We encounter many counterfeits of what we truly desire in the communion of saints, such as dating apps that promote casual sleeping around or the hook-up culture prevalent on many college campuses. Often when feeling the ache, we grasp for lower things that won't ever satisfy, or we try to find ways to numb the ache.

Sometimes our longing even causes us to turn the good icons of heavenly communion into idols. For example, if we fixate on the idea that a dating relationship or even marriage would resolve the ache of loneliness in our hearts, we may turn the icon of marriage into an idol. Instead, Christ invites us to offer Him our ache again and again, that He might fill us with hope for the communion of saints.

—⚬⚬—

Reflect

When was a time I had to leave a community or a group of friends that I loved?

Challenge

Next time you start to feel lonely, don't rush to distract yourself or "numb" the ache with food, noise, or busyness. Try paying attention to your longings and seek communion with God through your suffering. Allow Him to give you hope in the communion of saints. You might also use it as a time to reflect on your relationships: Which are not healthy? Which are icons of the love you are made for?

Pray

Lord Jesus, I am lonely. Don't leave me alone. Fill my heart and be present to me. Amen.

32

Friendship

by Brian Butler

"That's what love is, Adam.
When we choose to lay down our life for a friend."
- BRIDEGROOM

As previous stories have reflected, sometimes our choices for love can be dramatic. But more often than not, our choices to love are very mundane. What does laying down one's life for a friend actually look like in our ordinary experiences?

I think of Paul. Lisa and I had just moved our family an hour away to a new town. As we discerned the possibility of a permanent move, our temporary home was a one-bedroom apartment of just 340 square feet. With 3 kids ages 6 and under, we spent a memorable five months in what we dubbed, with ironic affection, the "Mega-Suite." After a particularly tough day, my friend Paul stopped by and surely noticed our kids bouncing off the walls. Soon after he left, two piping hot pizzas and some sodas were delivered to our door. Paul's simple, kind gesture saved the day as pepperoni and cheese turned our tiny space into a party.

I think of Kelley. I was annoyed when my friend Kelley noticed me making a sour-face and commented, "Why do you do that? You always make that face when you disagree or doubt something I say!" My wife jumped in, too. "That's it! He does that to me, too! I can't stand it!" After arguing a bit with them, I promised to pay more attention to my facial expressions. Over the next few weeks, I discovered I had a habit of wearing my disapproval of another's comments on my face in a condescending expression. Over time, and especially with help from Lisa, I was able to break this horrible habit. Kelley's bold friendship had challenged me to grow in kindness.

I think of Adam. When he went on a pilgrimage to Poland, he visited the places where my hero, St. John Paul II, grew up. Adam bought me a rosary but then kicked the gift up a notch; he carried the rosary everywhere he visited and prayed for me at each holy site. When Adam got back, he gave me a card detailing the prayerful journey of the rosary. He also did this same thing for Lisa and each of our kids. This intentional, beautiful gift revealed a true friend.

I have been truly *loved* by good friends laying down their lives for me in different ways. I once heard a radio-preacher say, "Love is not butterflies in your stomach. It's the dancin' in your feet." Real love offers surprise pizzas, admonishing challenges, prayerful pilgrimages, and much more. It is ordering one's masculine or feminine energy, time, and resources to serve the good of another, rather than giving on our own terms. It is listening well when you really want to talk. It is serving justice when required. It is mercy and forgiveness when they are not deserved. It is the corporal and spiritual works of mercy. Few things are more difficult or rewarding than excellent friendship. As Scripture tells us, "A faithful friend is a sturdy shelter; he that has found one has found a treasure" (Sir 6:14).

Do you want to know how well you love? Look no further than how well you make a gift of yourself, risking and sacrificing for others. How well do you imitate the One who said, "Whoever wishes to be great among you shall be your servant . . . the Son of Man did not come to be served but to serve and to give his life as a ransom for many" (Mt 20:26–28)?

—✺—

Reflect

Do I work intentionally on laying down my life each day? How do I treat the friends God has placed in my life?

Challenge

Ask God to bring to mind a friend for whom He wants you to lay down your life today or in the coming week. The less comfortable and more inconvenient the "laying down," the more likely you are actually fulfilling the demands of true love. Stay alert, and when you notice a need, do all you can to meet it.

Pray

Lord Jesus, I want to become a faithful friend, giving the best of myself, preferring the good of others over myself. Help me to give generously, serve humbly, and grow in authentic love. Amen.

33

Embracing the Body

by Joey Martineck

"Their bodies are not dirty."

- BRIDEGROOM

Have you ever overcorrected when driving to avoid a crash? While on one hand you are trying to dodge a real danger, overcorrecting on the road can be just as deadly. To avoid crashing into a deer, many have unfortunately driven off the road entirely and crashed instead into the trees.

We can often treat our desires for sex and intimacy in the same way. Confronted with the shame of some impure relationships in high school, I spent much of the later part of my life "overcorrecting" when it came to purity. Subconsciously, I began to regard sexual attraction and desire as "unholy." After all, my attractions are what got me into trouble in the first place, right? So instead of indulging in my desires like I had before, I began repressing them.

For many years I lived in this self-reliant mode of repression until I encountered Christopher West's book *Fill These Hearts*. As I sat in a little chapel reading the first few pages, I wept. I saw for the first time that Jesus was inviting me into something better than "overcorrecting" my past mistakes through rigorism; He was inviting me into healing.

Like I did, many of us have fallen for the heresy of Manichaeism, which basically teaches that the spirit is good while the body is bad. According to the Manichean, all things in the material world—including the body and natural, bodily desires—should be regarded with suspicion and contempt.[54]

At times, it sounds like Manichaeism might be in tune with the Christian soundtrack. Even St. Paul says that "if you live according to the flesh, you will die, but if by the Spirit you put to death the deeds of the body, you will live" (Rom 8:13). We ought to remember, however, that Paul is speaking to an audience long before Descartes proposed a different view of the human person. We are not souls trapped in a body, as Descartes suggested; we are enfleshed spirits (body-soul composites). Therefore, when the Bible speaks of the "flesh," it refers to fallen man's inclination to sin in body and soul, otherwise known as concupiscence.

Though sin has left us wounded, "man cannot stop at casting the 'heart' into a state of continual and irreversible suspicion."[55] Jesus saves us not by annihilating our humanity, but by entering in and transforming it. To live according to the Spirit is to experience the redemption of the body—and redemption of desire!—that Christ freely offers those who follow him.

—⁂—

Reflect

How do I regard my body? Am I guilty of having a hatred for bodily-ness?

Challenge

The next time the temptation to lust arises in your heart, instead of trying to distract yourself or repressing the desire, try exposing the desire before Jesus. Don't try to clean it up first: Jesus can handle it. If it is helpful, repeatedly say to Jesus "Look at me! Look at me!" to avoid concealing anything from Him. Also, consider praying the prayer below.

Pray (when lust arises)

Lord Jesus, in your name, I command this lustful thought to stand before you and be judged by you. This is your battle, Jesus. I place all my desires—twisted though they may be—at the foot of your cross and ask that your Holy Spirit would untwist them, giving new form to my strongest desires. Our Lady Undoer of Knots, pray for us. Amen.

34

The Shepherd's Voice

by Brian Butler

"What am I supposed to be hearing?"

- ADAM

With his background in archaeology, Father Harry was excited to be spending a few weeks of the summer working on an archaeological dig in Israel. One evening, he took a long walk across the foothills of the very mountains where God had called Moses, Jeremiah, and others in the Old Testament to be leaders and prophets for Him.

As he topped a hill, Father Harry saw shepherds herding their sheep into the small valley below. Without tags or branding, hundreds of sheep made their way from the hillsides into one large holding area. Father Harry wondered: *How will the shepherds know which ones belong to them?* Curious, he resolved to return the next day to watch the drama unfold.

Early the next morning, Father Harry perched himself on the hillside above the sheepfold. When the shepherds arrived below, they opened the gate and each began to sing and walk away from the pen. The sheep flooded out, forming lines as they followed their respective shepherds in different directions. Father Harry's shock gave way to wonder as the answer dawned on him. *The shepherds had been singing throughout each day to their sheep, guiding them, and keeping them familiar with their voices.* Jesus' words echoed in Father Harry's heart in a new way: "The sheep hear his voice as he calls his own by name and leads them out . . . the sheep follow him because they recognize his voice . . . I am the Good Shepherd. I know my sheep and my sheep know me" (Jn 10:3, 4, 14).

Jesus Himself set the example for how to hear God's voice. Pope Benedict XVI encouraged us, noting:

> The Gospels often present Jesus, especially at times of crucial decisions, withdrawing to lonely places, away from the crowds and even from the disciples in order to pray in silence . . . Silence can carve out an inner space in our very depths to enable God to dwell there, so that his word will remain within us and love for him take root in our minds and hearts and inspire our life. Hence the first direction: relearning silence, openness to listening, which opens us to the other, to the word of God.[56]

We must "relearn" silence in order to listen this attentively. If we do so, we will not only distinguish God's voice from the rest, but we'll even hear Him singing over us! "The Lord, your God, is in your midst, a mighty savior, Who will rejoice over you with gladness, and renew you in his love, Who will sing joyfully because of you" (Zeph 3:17). Like the sheep, we'll come to know our name as we hear it sung over us by our Shepherd. Then, God's word "will remain within us," and our love for Him can take root and inspire love in our lives.

—⟋⟍—

Reflect

How much intentional silence do I have in every day and every week? Have I trained the ear of my heart to listen for God's voice?

Challenge

Take a "desert-day" experience of silence. If you can't take a whole day, try a half day, or even just an hour of silence. No music. No books. No online browsing. No phone with all its constant notifications. Put everything aside and listen with the ear of your heart for the words of the One who is calling your name to lead you out into a new field of life.

Pray

Father, help me to learn to be silent, to listen that I may hear You singing over me and calling me by name. Help me to know that I am yours and to live from this reality. Amen.

35

When God Doesn't Answer the Way We Want

by Joey Martineck

"Let's call this: Rose"

- ADAM

A popular devotion to St. Therese of Lisieux, nicknamed "The Little Flower," asks the saint to send a rose as a sign of her intercession. Thousands of people around the world have experienced this sign of a rose as an encouragement to trust in God's love and providence. As I began transitioning from my sales career to discern priesthood, I too asked St. Therese for her prayers to confirm that I was on the right path and that God was with me.

During this same period, my friends Andrew and Carrie hosted a small house concert featuring Greg and Lizzy Boudreaux. I had heard Greg and Lizzy's music before, but experiencing it live in an intimate setting with close friends was particularly special. I bought their album *To the Dust* that night.

Toward the end of the show, the phone tucked in my pocket started vibrating. At first I ignored it, but the phone kept ringing, so I stepped outside to answer it. My brother immediately picked up.

"Grampy just died," he said.

Preparing to leave my career and my social community in Indianapolis as I moved toward priesthood was already weighing heavy on my heart. The news about Grampy broke my emotional dam.

As I ventured back inside the house, sharing my grief and receiving comfort from my friends, another woman whom I had only met that night approached me.

"I think this belongs to you," she said, and handed me a single red rose. She hadn't known anything about my ongoing prayer to St. Therese.

Sometimes God doesn't answer prayer the way we want. He often speaks through loss and suffering. Grampy's death was not how I wanted to receive a rose. Yet in that moment of sorrow, it reminded me that God was indeed close. With vivid conviction, I began to imagine Grampy experiencing the Song of Songs. Our ultimate destiny in Heaven—something that my friends and I were just singing about—suddenly became very real and a living truth.

A few days later, I was driving to Mass and listening to *To the Dust* in my car. Halfway there, the album's progression of the songs and the lyrics triggered a burst of inspiration. I saw very clearly a story hidden in Greg and Lizzy's music, a story that the world desperately needed to hear. We now call this story: *GARDEN*.

—⁓—

Reflect

When have I experienced a prayer that wasn't answered the way I wanted it to be? What was my response to this experience? What did it teach me about trusting God's plan?

Challenge

Pick a mundane part of your routine (driving to work, doing laundry, or the like) and use that time to cultivate awareness of God's presence. Often just intentionally being aware of God is the critical factor to transforming an ordinary day into something meaningful and fruitful. Pay attention to the "roses" he sends you as reminders that he is with you.

Pray

Lord Jesus, I ask that you answer my prayers. But even if you don't answer them exactly as I want, I trust that you are providing for me and loving me in ways I can't even imagine. Amen.

36

The Presentation

by Brian Butler

"To me, you'll always be my baby girl."

- BRIDEGROOM

Our daughter, Lauren, screamed for the first six months of her life due to colic. One Sunday during a summer vacation, we attended Mass at the cathedral in Charleston, South Carolina. Baby Lauren did not care that the music was beautiful or that we had chosen to sit too close to the front. During the readings, she cried so profusely that I moved her to the back of the church where I paced back and forth and tried to distract her with a combination of stained glass windows and the plastic rattle she insisted on throwing to the floor.

As I struggled to pray, the liturgy progressed and preparation began at the back of the church for the Presentation of the Gifts. This is the moment when we, the lay people, process up the aisle and present our simple gifts of bread and wine to the priest. He receives these gifts to be used in the next part of Mass, when he offers the prayer of consecration that changes those gifts into the body and blood of Jesus.

As Lauren screamed on, the procession headed toward the altar. As the consecration was about to make Jesus truly present among us, Lauren suddenly stopped crying. I bent over and helped her stand up. As she did so, she held my pointer fingers with her little hands and locked her big blue eyes on mine. She never looked more radiant than at that moment in her pink frilly dress, and as she gazed up at me, she broke into a toothless smile. Her beauty captivated me. As the organ music played and we stood at the rear of the center aisle, I had my first dance with my little daughter. Her little feet in white sandals pitter-pattered with joy and her thin, dark ringlets bounced around on her head as she pranced to the music floating through the 19th century church.

I suddenly realized that God was giving *me* a profound gift. I focused intensely on my daughter—struck by the reality that I may one day stand with her at the back of a church on her wedding day or on the day she becomes a bride of Christ. Again, an organ will play and a hushed crowd will await with the bridegroom for the presentation of the gift. On that day, Lauren herself will be the gift to be received, and to be presented by me—her father. I suddenly realized I needed years of preparation to be ready for such a profound moment: the presentation of my daughter *as a gift*.

If she chooses to follow a common custom, perhaps at her reception I will have another dance with my daughter. And during that special moment, when spectators wonder what the father of the bride whispers in his daughter's ear, I will tell Lauren a story. I will tell her of a cathedral, angelic music, the pitter-patter of little feet, and a Dad who fell in love with his baby girl.[57]

—⁂—

Reflect #1

How do I see myself in the eyes of God, the Father? How do I see all the sons and daughters whom the Father has entrusted to my love?

Reflect #2

Read and meditate on the prophet Isaiah's words, "For the Lord delights in you . . . And as a bridegroom rejoices in his bride, so shall your God rejoice in you" (Is. 62:4–5).

Challenge #1

Consider how God the Father first presented the gift of His daughter Eve to Adam and how He first presented the gift of His son Adam to Eve. Do you present yourself to the eyes of others with similar reverence and intentionality? If you have children, do you ensure that they present themselves to others in this way? What steps can you take to be more responsible with this profound gift?

Challenge #2

To dive deeper, read St. John Paul II's reflection on what ensures the true "exchange of the gift" of persons via the body and discover what might extort that gift (See TOB 17:3).

Pray

Our Father—my Father—help me to present myself and the others in my care to the eyes of others as the true gifts we are, always seeing ourselves through your eyes. Amen.

37

Control

by Joey Martineck

"And you wanna be the one who's in control"

- SERPENT

One summer I was sent to a Spanish immersion program in Guatemala as my summer seminarian assignment. After many days of firm discipline over my diet, I relaxed a bit and ate some *lechuga* (lettuce). Immediately, I became seriously ill. I couldn't help beating myself up for not being more cautious with food.

When I texted my mom an update, I expected a soft reprimand. She had warned me about lettuce specifically, because it is often sprayed with unclean water in developing countries. But there were no "I told you so's" from her. No shaming. Just her being present with me, as much as she could from miles away.

At the end of our text conversation, I said, "Thanks for being there." She responded with one word: "Always." Her love left no doubt in my mind that my mom—who can barely endure camping—would not have hesitated to fly down to a third world country if I had needed it.

Her love was bigger than my mistake. God's love, too, is bigger than our mistakes—not only our sins, but even our non-sinful human failures (like eating bad *lechuga*). If we offer both kinds of these mistakes to God, He can work all of them for good.

The Easter Vigil opens with a chant called the "Exsultet." It contains an interesting phrase concerning humanity's biggest mistake (the Fall of man and woman): "Oh happy fault, that earned so great, so glorious a Redeemer!" The Church is proclaiming that Christ's supreme act of love for us on the cross came about because of the worst sin of humanity. God can make our faults "happy."

This idea may, at first glance, seem confusing. Does this mean we should "sin that grace may abound" (Rom 6:1)? No! We must avoid sin, but put confidence in God's love instead of in our own power. The world often pressures us to control every aspect of our lives, leading many into anxiety-riddled perfectionism that is paralyzing and destructive in its own way. Entrusting our lives to God and accepting our failures in light of His providence and love can bring us deep healing. His love can "make all things new" (Rev 21:5).

—✠—

Reflect
What area of my life do I need to surrender control?

Challenge
Pray the beautiful Litany of Trust. You can find it on the website of the Sisters of Life: https://www.sistersoflife.org/litany-of-trust.

Pray
Lord Jesus, you know every hair on our heads. Thank you for knowing all the concerns in my heart at this moment. I entrust everything to you—especially my mistakes and disappointments. Let your kingdom come. Amen.

38

New Life

by Brian Butler

"But even now as we speak, new life grows in Eve's womb."

- BRIDEGROOM

It was 1994, and I had just tried out as a "walk-on" for the football team at the University of Colorado in Boulder. I didn't make the team, but the coaches invited me to work out with the team and plan to try out again the following spring. I was a place-kicker, and though much of my practice was on my own, I worked out daily in the team's fitness facility overlooking the stadium. That's where I met Rae Carruth.

Rae was an explosively fast wide-receiver, but I knew him as a workout partner. He was quiet and cocky but not mean. An English major, he once surprised me by reciting a poem in between reps on a bench press. Three years later, the Carolina Panthers drafted him as a first round pick and he signed a multi-million dollar contract. Carruth made an immediate impact on the field, but his off-field choices would make him infamous for years to come.

In 1999, Rae's girlfriend, Cherica Adams, became pregnant with their son. Rae tried to convince her to have an abortion, but Cherica refused, determined to have the baby. Six months later, Adams called 9-1-1 late one night after she was shot four times by a hired gunman. That night, she gave emergency birth to a little boy. A month later, Cherica Adams died, but her son, Chancellor, lived and was raised by his grandmother, Saundra Adams. Due to a lack of blood and oxygen caused by the shooting, Chancellor suffered brain damage and has cerebral palsy. Though Rae had run one of the fastest 40-yard dashes in NFL history, his son has had to fight hard to take every step.

Police arrested Rae Carruth for his role in hiring the gunman who killed Cherica. Following a high profile court case, Rae was convicted on three counts: discharging a firearm into occupied property, using an instrument with intent to destroy an unborn child, and conspiracy to commit murder. He spent more than 18 years in prison before being released on October 22, 2018.

Often, we remember dramatic and disturbing headlines but forget a story's real heroes and what we can learn from them. From Chancellor's first heartbeat, he was thrust into a battle between life and death. Cherica chose life and protected Chancellor while he was still growing within her, and then her mother, Saundra, faithfully raised her grandson. Though one man tried to destroy life, two good women made the sacrifices necessary to save it. Their sacrifices brought life from evil.

After the Fall, Adam and Eve's descendants struggle against all sorts of evils, but God is never thwarted from bringing about good. As the Genesis account records, Joseph's brothers try to kill him and eventually sell him into slavery. When Joseph eventually meets his brothers, he proclaims "you meant evil against me, but God meant it for good" (Gen 50:20).

Though Rae never even offered a simple apology, Saundra Adams says she long ago forgave him for his role in her daughter's death and grandson's challenges. Saundra's heroic love proves the Scripture: "The light shines in the darkness, and the darkness has not overcome it" (Jn 1:5). Meanwhile, Chancellor has grown into a young man whose smile brings joy to many; he and Saundra now live simply and he joins her as she make presentations to prisoners, educating and raising awareness on the nature of domestic violence.

Saundra Adams' faith fueled her forgiveness and helped her to love the smallest and most vulnerable, raising him into a strong young man. Saundra and Chancellor remind us that even thousands of years after Eden, even when we are surrounded by sin and death in the human family, God still brings forth new life.

—⚭—

Reflect

How do I treat the weakest and most vulnerable in my family and my community?

Challenge

Seek out those who have been violated in some way in your community. Pray for wisdom and then offer them life (spiritually, physically, emotionally, financially) in whatever way they need it most.

Pray

Jesus, help me to reverence the life of every single human being, no matter their age, race, religion or circumstances, especially those who are most vulnerable and defenseless. Help me forgive anyone in my life who does violence to those they should be protecting. Amen.

39

The Final Marriage

by Brian Butler

"You're made for the song of songs."

~ BRIDEGROOM

When I was young, I was captivated by the strength and beauty of many religious sisters. But I also wondered whether they were "missing out" by forgoing the gift of marriage. Today, I rarely encounter a "Sister Mary Bitter." But whenever I do, I pray for her. On the other hand, I am absolutely mystified by a "Sister Mary Joyful," and her life invites me to ponder: *what's behind the 'veil of her love' that makes her who she is?*

Rita Rizzo was born in Canton, Ohio in 1923. Her father abandoned the family when Rita was five. Her childhood was filled with difficulty, sickness, and the struggles of a depressed single mother. But they always prayed together. When Rita suffered a severe stomach illness and nearly died, they prayed a special prayer for nine days (called a novena), and on the ninth day Rita was cured. She fell in love with Jesus and promised Him great things. When she turned 21, Rita secretly entered the cloistered convent as a Poor Clare, taking the new name of Mary Angelica of the Annunciation. She left behind a note for her mother, saying, "If I were to ask your permission, you would never have granted it . . . I wanted you to give me to Our Lord as His Spouse . . . but this is His holy will."[58]

Thus began Sister Mary Angelica's new life of intimacy with Jesus. The relationship was tested by suffering yet strengthened in prayer, especially in Eucharistic Adoration, throughout 72 years of fidelity to her Spouse as a bride of Christ. Through suffering and adventure, providence and persistence, Sister Mary Angelica eventually became Mother Mary Angelica of the Annunciation and founded her own monastery. Later, she felt called to establish a cable TV network to help average Catholics grow in their faith.

Fueled with her fiery spirit and radical faith, in 1980 Mother Angelica began with a garage, $200, and zero broadcast experience. Eventually this beginning grew into the Eternal Word Television Network (EWTN), which today reaches millions globally. Along the way, Mother Angelica certainly walked by faith and not sight. At one point, she ordered a transponder that pushed her community's debt over a million dollars. She needed a $600,000 down payment to have the equipment dropped off, but even as the delivery truck rolled onsite, she knew they did not have the money. Mother Angelica retreated to the chapel to chat with her Spouse about the matter. Exactly at that moment, a man called the convent from his yacht in the Bahamas to say that after reading one of her booklets, he wanted to donate $600,000 to her. "Can you send it right now?" she asked. By lunchtime, the money was wired, the transponder delivered, and with another miracle complete, the network grew.[59] Through EWTN, she delivered the Catholic faith with humor and passion and became famous for insightful, sassy one-liners such as "Faith is one foot on the ground, one foot in the air, and a queasy feeling in the stomach."[60]

Through the years, various saints have asked for the Song of Songs to be read to them on their deathbeds. This Old Testament book presents dramatic romantic poetry exchanged between a human bridegroom and his bride, yet its spousal language has been long understood as an analogy of the exchange between God and His beloved. I don't know if Mother Angelica heard these Scripture passages in her final days, but she died trusting her Divine Bridegroom on March 27, 2016.

Her joyful celibacy and sincere gift of self showed the vitality of a *spiritual* marriage that began on earth and bore innumerable spiritual children. She knew that "missing out" on *sacramental* marriage on earth was like passing a water fountain in order to drink from the freshwater spring that is its source. Even more so than the witness of her powerful confidence in God's providence, consecrated men and women like Mother Angelica have an inherent sign value. They point us to heaven—the destiny for which we are all created.

—∿∿—

Reflect

What shapes my vision of what I see as my final communion with Jesus? How can those who live joy-filled celibacy help orient my own heart to live for my own 'final marriage'? How can I change my life so I, too, can become a joy-filled sign of heaven?

Challenge

Identify a joyful celibate person —priest, sister, brother, or consecrated lay person—who lives near you (ask around if necessary). Invite him or her for dinner or coffee, and have a deep conversation about the meaning of life.

Pray

Lord, help me see your desire for me to be with you forever. Give me the grace to keep my eyes open today to see how you are pointing me to a mysterious and joyful eternity as a member of the Bride of Christ, the Church, in the final marriage. Amen.

40

The Consecration

by Brian Butler

"Oh happy fault, that gained for us so great a savior."
- BRIDEGROOM

My brother, Timmy, was 22 months old when my mom tucked him into his bed one night and shut off the light. She started to leave the room but sensed a gentle leading of the Holy Spirit to re-consecrate Timmy to the Blessed Virgin Mary's protection. Although she had done so before, she nonetheless returned to Timmy's crib and entrusted her son again to the love and maternity of Mary.

The next morning, Timmy was accidentally run over by a pickup truck. The impact fell directly over his abdomen, breaking his spleen into two pieces and slashing open his liver. As they opened up his body for emergency surgery, the doctors were shocked to find that Timmy's spleen had clotted. They told my parents that he could have bled to death before ever reaching the hospital. Just a few days later, Timmy was jumping off of furniture like active little boys do, and on his way to full health. Every Thanksgiving since then, my parents set aside time to reflect again on this event and give special thanks to God for Timmy's miraculous healing.

Purposefully retelling stories like this occurs throughout our spiritual life, extending back through salvation history. The Jews gather each year on the feast of Passover to remember God's faithfulness to them millennia ago in Egypt. The Passover prayer begins with the youngest child asking, "Why is tonight different than all other nights?" Then, the gathered community retells the story of their salvation: God saved them from death through each family slaughtering an unblemished lamb, putting its blood across their doorposts, and then eating its flesh. These actions signaled the angel of death to "pass over" that home and spare the first-born sons within.

Catholics also gather to retell the story of God's faithfulness. Each year at the Easter vigil Mass, a special hymn-prayer called the "Exsultet" is sung acapella by a lone vocalist in the darkened Church. The song tells a hauntingly beautiful story that points back to the Garden of Eden, recounting God's fidelity to His people and offering the key phrase, *"O happy fault that earned so great, so glorious a Redeemer!"* This prayer was the inspiration for Greg and Lizzy Boudreaux to write the Bridegroom's lyrics above.

The poetry couldn't be more dramatic! The first Adam sinned, ushering death into the world, but his fault won for us the Father's decision to send a *new Adam* to reconcile man's infidelity. How? Through radical fidelity, abandoning Himself in the Garden of Gethsemane to the Father's will, Christ was obedient unto death. Instead of picking the fruit *off* the tree, Jesus became the fruit *on* the tree—the tree of the cross. On that night before He died, Jesus instituted the Sacrament of the Eucharist to *feed* us Himself. Then, after dying and rising three days later, Jesus conquered death and set us on a path towards Heaven. And all of this flows through Mary, who said *yes* with her whole body and soul. Blessed is she among women, and blessed is the *fruit* of her womb, Jesus.

But this beautiful poetry is actually the true, living drama of our salvation story that began in Eden, runs through Gethsemane, and culminates in Heaven. In this way, Jesus Christ, "the final Adam, by the revelation of the mystery of the father and his love, fully reveals man to man himself and makes his supreme calling clear."[61]

There is a famous verse in Genesis known as the *protoevangelium* (meaning "first Gospel"). Here, the Lord curses the serpent, sentencing him to forever slither on his belly, and then says "I will put enmity between you and the woman, and between your seed and her seed; he shall bruise your head and you shall bruise his heel" (Gen 3:15, RSV-CE). This is God's incredible response of love to the plight of Adam and Eve's original sin! Instead of leaving them to save themselves, He promises to send them a Savior.

The *protoevangelium* is the first foreshadowing of the Messiah, the first foretelling of the Incarnation, and is a powerful reminder of God's desire for union with us, His people. Immediately after the Fall, the Father begins revealing His plan to restore our union by sending His only son to crush the head of the serpent, so that all the children of Adam and Eve may be saved.

What a gift and consolation these words must have been to Eve! With a mother's instinct to nurture and protect, Eve likely knew that danger would lurk daily now for her children. Though Eve sinned by distrusting the Father and disobeying His command, God did not cast the woman out of the story. Rather, He places woman at the very center.

Thousands of years later, in the fullness of time, He chose another woman—a young virgin—through whom He would send His Son to crush the serpent. Mary opened her entire being to God, entrusting herself to Him and proclaiming *fiat* *(yes)* to the angel Gabriel's proposal. With her total consecration of herself to God's will, the Virgin Mary became the "new Eve."

The act of consecration is not rocket-science. The word "consecrate" means to set apart. When God sets people apart, He gives special graces to sanctify them and enable them to perform a particular God-given mission. The Church teaches that Our Lady was conceived without original sin and, by her own cooperation with God's grace, remained free of all actual sin as part of her consecration. Why? God preserved her from sin so she could be a perfect vessel through which God's son could enter the world.

My mom is one of the best and most amazing mothers. By totally consecrating herself to Jesus through Mary, and then consecrating her children to Mary, my mom gave each of us a great opportunity—and for Timmy, maybe a second chance—to live totally set apart for the one Who promised us a Savior.

—⟋⟍—

Reflect

Do I recognize my need for a savior? Have I chosen to set myself apart for Christ?

Challenge

Take up a special devotion to Our Lady, the Blessed Virgin Mary. By doing a special act of entrustment called "Total Consecration" to Mary, in a 33-day set of prayers, you will launch deeper into the heart of Jesus through His mother. (See resources on page 121.)

Pray

Dear Mary, if I do not yet know you as my mother or know your son Jesus, please help me draw closer to you and to the One who came through you to become my Savior. Hail Mary . . . Amen.

Suggested Resources

MUSIC

To the Dust by Greg&Lizzy (Dumb Ox Ministries, 2013)
The musical album that inspired *GARDEN: The Musical.*

BOOKS

Catechism of the Catholic Church (Doubleday, 1994)
A comprehensive synthesis of the teachings of the Catholic Church.

Fill These Hearts: God, Sex, and the Universal Longing
by Christopher West (Image, 2013)
Explores what the desires for love, sex, and intimacy are about and
what they reveal about the destiny of humanity.

Love & Responsibility: New Translation
by Karol Wojtyla (Pauline Books and Media, 2013)
Considered the precursor to his TOB, this pre-papal classic by St.
John Paul II explains the nature of relationships, sexual desire, and
authentic love.

Man and Woman He Created Them: A Theology of the Body
by St. John Paul II. Translated by Michael Waldstein (Pauline Books
and Media, 2006)
The definitive text combining his TOB reflections, collectively known
as the Theology of the Body.

Men, Women, and the Mystery of Love by Edward Sri (Servant, 2015)
A resource for young adults on love, attraction, sexual desire, and
relationships breaks open Karol Wojtyla's *Love and Responsibility.*

Theology of the Body for Beginners
by Christopher West (Beacon Publishing, 2018)

Summarizes the primary insights of St. John Paul II's revolutionary teaching in a widely-accessible presentation.

Theology of His Body/Theology of Her Body
by Jason Evert (Ascension Press, 2009)
What do the male and female body reveal? How do they reveal our call to love? A readable book for teens and young adults.

Theology of the Body in One Hour
by Jason Evert (Totus Tuus Press, 2018)
Evert presents St. John Paul II's teachings in a quick-read format.

33 Days to Morning Glory
by Michael E. Gaitley, MIC (Marian Press, 2011)
An easy approach to Marian Consecration, offering a simple, 33-day format.

PROGRAMS & CURRICULA

YOU: Life, Love, and the Theology of the Body
by Brian Butler, Jason and Crystalina Evert (Ascension Press, 2016)
This program for teens makes St. John Paul II's teachings relatable. Adaptable for parish and school settings. Includes a leader's guide, student workbook, video content, and a parent guide.

Theology of the Body for Teens: Middle School Edition
by Brian Butler, Jason Evert, and Colin and Aimee MacIver (Ascension Press, 2011)
Created for middle school youth, this program is easily integrated into parish and school settings. Includes a leader's guide, student workbook, video content, and a parent guide.

ORGANIZATIONS

The Cor Project (corproject.com)
Christopher West and collaborators equip men and women to learn,

live, and share the beauty of the divine plan for human life, love, and sexuality in a new evangelization.

The Theology of the Body Institute (tobinstitute.org)
Spreads the message of Theology of the Body through graduate level courses, on-site speaker programs, and clergy enrichment training.

joyTOB: Proclaiming the Joy to BE (joytob.org)
Damon Owens joyfully shares the goodness, truth, and beauty of human sexuality and the call to love via lectures, motivational speaking, writing, and TV/radio presentations.

Into the Deep (idretreats.org)
Jen Messing facilitates understanding of our identity and dignity as persons made in the image of God through "identity-based retreats," seminars, study groups, and speaking.

ECHO Theology of the Body Camps (dumboxministries.com)
ECHO is Dumb Ox Ministries' flagship, immersive experience in St. John Paul II's Theology of the Body for teens and young adults. The TOB is presented in dynamic ways and experienced through authentic community.

Ruah Woods (ruahwoods.org)
Located in Ohio, this TOB education center offers classes, retreats, discipleship programs, speakers, psychological services aimed at holistic healing, and school curricula.

Courage (couragerc.org)
Courage members are men and women who experience same-sex attraction and who have made a commitment to strive for chastity.

Eden Invitation (edeninvitation.com)
An organization dedicated to providing support and community to young adults experiencing same-sex attraction.

BLOGS & WEBSITES

The Porn Effect (theporneffect.com)
The Porn Effect aims to expose the reality behind the fantasy of pornography and to equip individuals to find freedom from porn use.

Fight the New Drug (fightthenewdrug.org)
Using science, facts, and personal accounts, FTND is a non-religious, non-legislative organization that helps people make educated decisions about pornography.

Chastity Project (chastity.com)
Founded by Jason and Crystalina Evert, this leading chastity resource offers speaking, blogs, and digital and print media that empowers young people to embrace chastity and true love.

Made In His Image (madeinhisimage.org)
Provides a safe and compassionate setting for dialogue, discussion and education that fosters healing for women suffering from eating disorders or physical or sexual abuse.

CHURCH DOCUMENTS

Familiaris Consortio: On the Role of the Christian Family in the Modern World (St. John Paul II, 1981)

Humanae Vitae: On Human Life (St. Paul VI, 1968)

Mulieris Dignitatem: On the Dignity and Vocation of Women (St. John Paul II, 1988)

Salvifici Doloris: On the Christian Meaning of Human Suffering (St. John Paul II, 1984)

The Truth and Meaning of Human Sexuality: Guidelines for Education within the Family (Pontifical Council for the Family, 1995)

GARDEN: The Musical

GARDEN is an original musical play written by Joey Martineck, featuring the music of Greg and Lizzy Boudreaux and was originally produced by Dumb Ox Ministries. A full-stage retelling of the story of Adam and Eve in the Garden of Eden, it is adapted from the book of Genesis with inspiration from the writings of St. John Paul II. The play features dialogue that balances humor and drama with a plot that is creatively surprising while being dynamically familiar. Themes of authentic love, relationship, and struggle inspire the audience with the truth of what it means to be human. *GARDEN* invites us to revisit what it means to be created from love; to consider our need for God's mercy; and to answer the call to live in true freedom.

**For *GARDEN* merchandise,
bulk discounts for this book,
or for *GARDEN* licensing info:
Please call Dumb Ox Ministries at (985) 951–2215.
www.GardenTheMusical.com**

Endnotes

1. G.K. Chesterton, quoted by Ann Voskamp, *One Thousand Gifts* (Zondervan: Grand Rapids, 2011), 131.
2. These short talks were mostly delivered in St. Peter's Square in Rome. The six undelivered talks were never given, but were discovered by Dr. Michael Waldstein in the Vatican vaults after the death of Pope John Paul II. Later, the talks were compiled into a compendium that is commonly called the "Theology of the Body." Technically, that is a subtitle, not the title of the work. For quick reference, we will use "TOB" to refer to this work in the end notes. Cf. Pope John Paul II, *Man and Woman He Created Them: A Theology of the Body, trans. Michael Waldstein* (Boston: Pauline Books and Media, 2006).
3. TOB 43:7.
4. *Catechism of the Catholic Church*, 2705.
5. *Catechism of the Catholic Church*, 2706.
6. St. Therese of Lisieux, quoted in *Catechism of the Catholic Church*, 2558.
7. *Catechism of the Catholic Church*, 221.
8. TOB 19:2.
9. Cf. TOB 19:2.
10. Pope John Paul II, *Letter to Women*, 4.
11. Stein, Edith, *Essays on Woman, Second Edition, trans. Freda Mary Oben* (Washington, DC: ICS Publications, 1996), 6.
12. *Gaudium et Spes*, 22.
13. *Catechism of the Catholic Church*, 1.
14. St. Teresa of Calcutta's letter, "I Thirst For You," is available at https://catholic-link.org/quotes/i-thirst-letter-written-mother-teresa-quote/.
15. *Catechism of the Catholic Church*, 2563.
16. Karol Wojtyla, *Love and Responsibility* (San Francisco: Ignatius Press, 1993) 135.
17. *Catechism of the Catholic Church*, 1749.
18. TOB 15:3.
19. TOB 46:6.
20. TOB 8:3.
21. TOB 6:2.
22. This was not solely a "male" experience. St. John Paul II was clear that original solitude was a fundamental *human* experience, an experience in which women share a common heritage with men. Cf. TOB 5:2.
23. Dave Roever, *Scarred* (Fort Worth, TX: Roever Communications, 1995), 42.
24. Ibid, 112.
25. TOB 102:5.
26. Christopher West. *Theology of the Body for Beginners: Rediscovering the Meaning of Life, Love, Sex, and Gender* (North Palm Beach: Beacon Publishing), 116.
27. What's the problem with pornography? In short, the problem with porn is not that it shows too much of the person, but that it shows too little of the person. The "actors" or "models" are reduced to their bodily values, in order to be used for another's sexual gratification. Pornography trains consumers to habitually separate sex from authentic self-gift, which is contrary to God's design. Porn damages the full dignity of the human person, and inhibits consumers' capacity for authentic, self-giving, and life-giving love. For more information about the problems with pornography, its effects, and how to break free from it, visit theporneffect.com, fightthenewdrug.com, or chastity.com.
28. Bansal A, Garg C, Pakhare A, Gupta S. "Selfies: A Boon or Bane?" *J Family Med Prim Care* [serial online] 2018 [cited 2018 Nov 2];7:828–31. Available from: http://www.jfmpc.com/text.asp?2018/7/4/828/240385.

29. TOB 5:5.
30. World Youth Day, *Homily*, Toronto, July 28, 2002.
31. Pope John Paul II, *Dies Domini*, 11.
32. TOB 43:7.
33. Cf. Christopher West. *Theology of the Body Explained: A Commentary on John Paul II's Gospel of the Body* (Gracewing: 2003), 170.
34. St. John Paul II taught the opposite of love is not hate, but *using* another person as a means to an end. Treating a person as a means to an end "does violence to the very essence of the other" by violating their dignity and right to determine their own ends (*Love and Responsibility*, 27). St. John Paul II went even further to describe what happens when a society uses its members via "utilitarianism." He notes, *"Utilitarianism is a civilization of production and of use, a civilization of 'things' and not of 'persons', a civilization in which persons are used in the same way as things are used. In the context of a civilization of use, woman can become an object for man, children a hindrance to parents, the family an institution obstructing the freedom of its members"* (*Letter to Families*, 13). It's easy fall into using another—even in marriage—where sometimes lust passes itself off as love. The good of commitment in marriage can veil weaknesses in communication and turn the marriage bed into a place where use masks itself as love. Such use can cause an erosion of love and when its mask is removed, we see the darkness for what it is. But the human heart knows it was made for love, not use. To learn more about the nature of St. John Paul II's rationale for love over use, see Edward Sri, *Men, Women and the Mystery of Love: Practical Insights from John Paul II's Love and Responsibility* (Servant, 2015).
35. TOB 114:6.
36. TOB 131:4.
37. St. Paul VI, *Humanae Vitae*, 12.
38. TOB 32:3.
39. Consider searching YouTube for videos on *Humanae Vitae* and/or contraception by Janet Smith, Jason Evert, or Christopher West.
40. TOB 32:6.
41. TOB 30:1.
42. TOB 13:1.
43. TOB 28:6.
44. TOB 32:3.
45. *Catechism of the Catholic Church*, 399.
46. Christopher West. *Theology of the Body for Beginners: Rediscovering the Meaning of Life, Love, Sex, and Gender, St. John Paul II Edition* (North Palm Beach: Beacon), 71.
47. *Catechism of the Catholic Church*, 397.
48. *Catechism of the Catholic Church*, 398.
49. *Gaudium et Spes*, 24.
50. *Catechism of the Catholic Church*, 405.
51. Pope John Paul II, *Novo Millenio Ineunte*, 32.
52. Ibid, 33.
53. TOB 68:4.
54. TOB 44:5–6, TOB 45:1–5.
55. TOB 46:4.
56. Pope Benedict XVI, *General Audience*, 7 March 2012.
57. The author's story first appeared on CatholicExchange.com in 2002.
58. Raymond Arroyo, *Mother Angelica: The Remarkable Story of a Nun, Her Nerve and a Network of Miracles,* (New York: Doubleday, 2005), 44.
59. Ibid, 158.
60. Ibid, 153.
61. *Gaudium et Spes*, 22.

AUTHORS

 Joey Martineck is the Director of Respect Life Ministry for the Archdiocese of Atlanta. He was a seminarian for three years at Notre Dame Seminary in New Orleans, LA, where he obtained a Bachelor's in Philosophy for Theological Studies. He also studied at the Theology of the Body Institute in Philadelphia, PA and the Institute for Priestly Formation in Omaha, NE. Joey has spoken to thousands on faith, human sexuality, and desire. He is the libretto writer of *GARDEN* the musical and writer of the one act play *Wise Men*.

 Brian Butler is the Executive Director of Dumb Ox Ministries. He has authored and contributed to numerous resources and programs, including *Theology of the Body for Teens: Middle School Edition* and the *YOU* program for teens. He is the original producer of *GARDEN* and the director of a feature-length reality film, *Mystery Trip*. Brian's bachelor's degree is in Communications and he holds a Masters in Theology. He has over 20 years of ministry experience, and is a popular speaker and trainer around the country. He and his wife, Lisa, reside in the New Orleans area with their four children.

ABOUT THE PUBLISHER

Dumb Ox Ministries is a 501 (c) 3 non profit organization that works with teens, young adults, and families, cultivating their authentic masculinity and femininity through the Theology of the Body, helping them to prepare for, discern, and pursue their unique vocations to love. Dumb Ox evangelizes thousands of people each year by facilitating group retreats and camps, parish missions, and diocesan events. They do outreach locally, regionally, and throughout the world through one-on-one mentoring, creative media, and dynamic speaking.